Living with Christ

2026–2027 MASS & PRAYER Journal

THIS JOURNAL BELONGS TO

Living with Christ

PUBLISHER: David Dziena
ASSOCIATE PUBLISHER: Brother Daniele Caglioni, A.A.
EDITOR: Terence Hegarty
PROJECT EDITOR: Michelle Gerstel
DESIGN: Jeff McCall

Sponsored by the Augustinians of the Assumption
PROVINCIAL: Father Chi Ai Nguyen, A.A.

Bayard USA
500 Salisbury St. ■ Worcester, MA 01609
PHONE: (800) 214-3386
WEBSITE: www.livingwithchrist.us
EMAIL: LWC@bayardfaithresources.com

ISBN: 978-1-62785-877-9
Printed in the U.S.A.

bayard

FSC www.fsc.org
MIX
Paper | Supporting responsible forestry
FSC® C005010

You are the

Body of Christ.

In you and through you
the work of the incarnation
must go forward.
You are to be taken.

**You are to
be blessed,**

broken, and distributed,
that you may be the means of grace
and the vehicles of eternal love.

ST. AUGUSTINE

WHY JOURNAL?

Spiritual journaling is a form of prayer. Far beyond recapping our life's events, the exercise of journaling helps us to express our spiritual life. Our written words capture our spiritual experiences, thoughts, struggles, victories—and essentially form a prayer through which we communicate to God what lies in our innermost self.

The exercise of spiritual journaling does not require us to be experienced in such a practice, nor are there any specific guidelines. When we journal, we need not worry about style or formalities. Just as in our regular prayers, Jesus wishes us to speak freely, simply, and honestly what is in our heart.

This journal provides a guideline to your prayer exercise in the **Responding to the Word** section each day, where you will find a question that is directly connected to the readings of the day. If this question is helpful, feel free to use it, but do not feel constrained by it.

Spiritual journaling will essentially enlarge our vision and lead to a greater understanding of our spiritual journey.

PRAYER *for the* HELP *of the* HOLY SPIRIT

Come, Holy Spirit,
fill the hearts of your faithful
and kindle in them the fire of your love.
Send forth your Spirit
and they shall be created,
and you shall renew the face of the earth.
O God, who by the light of the Holy Spirit,
did instruct the hearts of the faithful,
grant that by the same Holy Spirit
we may be truly wise
and ever enjoy his consolations.
Through the same Christ Our Lord.

AMEN.

SUNDAY **NOVEMBER 29**

1ST SUNDAY *of* ADVENT

After fifty years of bitter exile in Babylon, the children of Israel returned home. Their time away was one of yearning and dreaming, of anticipating and hungering, of longing and thirsting for that which was lost. But their promised land was now reduced to a few square miles under a Persian governor. Jerusalem lay in ruins, as did the other towns and villages. The fields lay undisturbed under their blanket of weeds. In his "Psalm of Entreaty" the prophet begs God to "rend the heavens" and come to the aid of his people.

We can identify with this post-exilic people, can't we? We are all too aware of what has been wrought by choices made throughout the expanse of history: war and violence, fear and suffering, hunger, homelessness and exile. Despite all the advances made by human ingenuity, our praying and sacrificing, it all seems to remain the same. Like Israel, we know the disappointment.

Isaiah recalls the tenderness that God, the divine potter, shows to us, the work of his hands. Paul gently reminds us that we have been enriched in innumerable ways by the grace of God at work in us and through us, such that we lack no spiritual good. The Lord Jesus himself urgently calls us to stay awake. Stay awake for what? Stay awake for his return: a visitation that surprises and delights us in the sheer unexpected nature of God's coming into our lives. **REV. ROGER KEELER**

PEOPLE AND PRAYERS TO REMEMBER THIS WEEK

Responding *to the* Word

Jesus warns us to "watch" and be alert. ***What makes me less attentive to God's presence than I want?***

READINGS OF THE DAY

Isaiah 63:16b-17, 19b; 64:2-7

Psalm 80

1 Corinthians 1:3-9

Mark 13:33-37

Final Thoughts...

FEASTS THIS WEEK

November 30: **St. Andrew**

December 3: **St. Francis Xavier**

December 4: **St. John Damascene**

SUNDAY **DECEMBER 6**

2ND SUNDAY *of* ADVENT

The way that led to Christian faith in Jesus Christ as savior and God-with-us was prepared in the covenant relationship between Israel and its God. Israel understood itself as having been justly judged yet fully forgiven by God for its sins and restored to life when its people's hearts—and cities—lay in ruins. Out of this "nothingness," God spoke a powerful and effective word of comfort, deliverance, and loving-kindness.

Prophets heralded these good tidings and psalmists sang about them: God would imbue the earth with steadfast love, faithfulness, righteousness, and peace—divine attributes that can seem so elusive in human life. One particular figure in Israel's history—John the Baptist—facilitated the people's repentance in preparing for God's arrival, in his life and death pointing others toward Jesus. Apostles were chosen; a church was formed which awaited the return of the risen Lord in glory.

But the wait became a long one, and Christians and their God became the source of ridicule. In response, faithful disciples proclaimed anew that God remains sovereign and Other, yet incarnate also, and so profoundly loving toward us as to wait in hope for each one to embrace righteous living and the gift of salvation. May such patience in our God arouse us to gratitude and renewed fervor this Advent! **CHRISTINE MADER**

Responding *to the* Word

Isaiah encourages us to prepare the way of the Lord. ***What preparations can I make to invite Jesus to be more present in my life this week?***

PEOPLE AND PRAYERS TO REMEMBER
THIS WEEK

READINGS
OF THE DAY

Isaiah 40:1-5, 9-11

Psalm 85

2 Peter 3:8-14

Mark 1:1-8

Final Thoughts...

FEASTS THIS WEEK

December 7: **St. Ambrose**

December 8: **Immaculate Conception of the Blessed Virgin Mary**

December 9: **St. Juan Diego Cuauhtlatoatzin**

December 10: **Our Lady of Loreto**

December 11: **St. Damasus I**

December 12: **Our Lady of Guadalupe**

TUESDAY **DECEMBER 8**

THE IMMACULATE CONCEPTION *of the* BLESSED VIRGIN MARY

The people of Israel expected God to intervene in human history at some point, to establish peace over the nation. Whereas they were hoping for a kingly and triumphant Messiah who would overthrow their enemies through power and might, a little baby was born in a stable with a mission to establish a kingdom of love and mercy through gentleness, humility, and service to neighbor.

Jesus did not meet their expectations. But perhaps we can argue that in some way Jesus exceeded their expectations, even if it was somewhat difficult to make sense of it all.

I imagine it was a surprise to Mary as well. As a devout young woman, she surely desired a relationship with God, just like any other devout person of her day. But she likely had not expected that God would become present in her life in the way that the birth, life, and death of Christ was to unfold.

Has God ever exceeded your expectations? Have you ever prayed for something and found that your prayer was answered, but not in the way that you imagined? Was the outcome difficult to accept?

The *yes* that God awaits from us in response has the potential to radically transform our reality into far more than we ever hoped for. Let us pray for Mary's heroic courage and generosity of heart to allow God to work in our lives as well. **NATALIA KONONENKO**

PEOPLE AND PRAYERS TO REMEMBER THIS WEEK

Responding *to the* Word

The angels tell Mary that nothing is impossible for God. ***What miracles have I experienced in my life by God's powerful intervention?***

READINGS OF THE DAY

Genesis 3:9-15, 20

Psalm 98

Ephesians 1:3-6, 11-12

Luke 1: 26-38

Final Thoughts...

SUNDAY **DECEMBER 13**

3RD SUNDAY *of* ADVENT

What is the best preparation for Christmas? The gospel today gives us a hint that we might miss unless we listen carefully. Men asked John if he was the one whom they expected. Was he a prophet whose voice had been long silent in Israel? Or, perhaps, was he Messiah to a people longing for a redeemer? John knew he was not the one. Testifying to the coming of Jesus, he says that he was not fit to unstrap the sandals of the One who was coming. Rabbis of the day said that a disciple could do anything for his master *except* untie his sandals, a job too menial even for a disciple. What John means is that he is not even fit to be Jesus' slave. His humility—his self-forgetfulness—gives us a picture of a person who is prepared to welcome Jesus.

The same humility runs through the whole text. Earlier, John calls everyone to "*make straight the way of the Lord*," the work of subjects for a king. This preparation is a preparation of the heart. Preparing our hearts for Jesus means turning from ourselves—self-preoccupation—to God in Christ Jesus.

John is a model of this turning from ourselves to point to the One who is greater than we are, the One who is the true Redeemer. May God give us the grace to forget ourselves and to remember only Christ. **REV. JAMES B. SAUER**

PEOPLE AND PRAYERS TO REMEMBER THIS WEEK

READINGS OF THE DAY

Isaiah 61:1-2a, 10-11

Luke 1

1 Thessalonians 5:16-24

John 1:6-8, 19-28

Responding *to the* Word

Paul advises us not to quench the Holy Spirit. ***How have I been hesitant to let God's Spirit work in me this Advent?***

Final Thoughts...

FEASTS THIS WEEK

December 14: **St. John of the Cross**

SUNDAY **DECEMBER 20**

4TH SUNDAY *of* ADVENT

When I was a child, my parents would often tell me that the best present I could ever give them was to "just be good." This meant, among other things, always treating my younger siblings well—no matter what they did to me. Mom and Dad received some very short-lived presents. But what really mattered was my effort to please them, to respect and honor their wishes.

David strove to please God throughout his life. The second king of Judah and Israel ensured during his long reign that the Jewish people worshiped the one, true God and not false idols as they had in the past. David's close relationship with God is one that we should emulate during Advent, Christmastide, and throughout the new year ahead. When David sinned, he was quick to repent and make amends. He talked with God regularly, was dependent on God for everything, and tried to do God's will.

The same can be said of Mary. Conceived without sin, still Mary was born with free will. Our Blessed Mother could have said no to God's plans for her to give birth to his son. Instead, Mary chose to honor God with her life. In Mary we see what God can do with us, in us, and through us when we are open, listen to God's word, and trust in God's goodness. **PATRICIA TAKEDA**

PEOPLE AND PRAYERS TO REMEMBER
THIS WEEK

Responding *to the* Word

Mary gives herself completely to God's plans for her. ***What is God inviting me to do to share in Christ's work now?***

READINGS
OF THE DAY

2 Samuel 7:1-5, 8b-12, 14a, 16

Psalm 89

Romans 16:25-27

Luke 1:26-38

Final Thoughts...

FEASTS THIS WEEK

December 21: **St. Peter Canisius**
December 23: **St. John of Kanty**
December 25: **Nativity of the Lord**
December 26: **St. Stephen**

FRIDAY **DECEMBER 25**

THE NATIVITY *of the* LORD (CHRISTMAS)

Since the very first Christmas in Bethlehem, the birth of Christ has generated tremendous hope. Mary and Joseph coming to town for the census, the shepherds living in the area, the Magi traveling from the East—all of them have come to this place with the greatest expectations and hopes. These expectations and hopes are fulfilled beyond imagination: "The people who walked in darkness have seen a great light," proclaims Isaiah; "Do not be afraid; for behold, I proclaim to you good news of great joy that will be for all the people," the angel says to the shepherds.

Christmas is hope fulfilled. Christmas is joy proclaimed to the world. Christmas is "good news of great joy" because God has decided to dwell among us, to become one of us and share our joys and sorrows. Christmas manifests how much God cares for humankind and wishes to bring us comfort, peace, and salvation. Throughout the season of Advent, Christians have been awaiting the coming of the Messiah. It is now up to each one of us to share the light, the flame, and the hope generated by the birth of this God-child.

Let us pray on this solemn feast of Christmas for peace on earth. Let us pray that new hope and new reasons to rejoice may be granted to all humankind. Merry Christmas to all! **JEAN-PIERRE PRÉVOST**

PEOPLE AND PRAYERS TO REMEMBER THIS WEEK

READINGS OF THE DAY

Mass during the Night

Isaiah 9:1-6

Psalm 96

Titus 2:11-14

Luke 2:1-14

Mass at Dawn

Isaiah 62:11-12

Psalm 97

Titus 3:4-7

Luke 2:15-20

Mass during the Day

Isaiah 52:7-10

Psalm 98

Hebrews 1:1-6

John 1:1-18

Responding *to the* Word

Paul understands how accepting Christ means rejecting godless ways. ***What unhelpful behaviors have I rejected to follow Christ's ways?***

Final Thoughts...

HOLY FAMILY *of* JESUS, MARY, *and* JOSEPH

In family life, moments of joy can be counterbalanced by moments of confusion and pain we would like to forget. All these moments, however, offer families opportunities to grow and become stronger.

I'm not sure it was any easier for people of the ancient world to be a family, because the pressures they experienced were likely as overwhelming as some situations we face today. The Holy Family is often seen through an idealized lens, which might make it harder for us to relate to them. But like us, they, too, must have had their struggles. Joseph was a tradesman who depended on piecework to support his family. Mary may well have had to scrimp and save to make ends meet.

We know little of Jesus at this stage in his life. Yet no matter what challenges the family faced, Mary and Joseph supported Jesus in a way that enabled him to grow in age and grace and wisdom before God and others. Jesus experienced solidarity within the family, with those around him, and with God. He grew up in a loving community.

As we gather to celebrate and reflect upon family on this holy day, let our prayer be for solidarity as we feast at the table of the Lord. May this unity help us to grow in wisdom and grace before God and others. **ANTHONY CHEZZI**

PEOPLE AND PRAYERS TO REMEMBER THIS WEEK

Responding *to the* Word

Simeon and Anna rejoice because Jesus has come to them. ***How can I share with others the ways Jesus' presence has changed me and my life?***

READINGS OF THE DAY

Genesis 15:1-6; 21:1-3

Psalm 105

Hebrews 11:8, 11-12, 17-19

Luke 2:22-40

Final Thoughts...

FEASTS THIS WEEK

December 28: **Holy Innocents**

December 29: **St. Thomas Becket**

December 31: **St. Sylvester I**

January 1: **Mary, the Holy Mother of God**

January 2: **St. Basil the Great & St. Gregory Nazianzen**

FRIDAY **JANUARY 1**

MARY, *the* **HOLY MOTHER** *of* **GOD**

World Day of Peace

When my wife was pregnant, we couldn't agree on a name to give our child. Luckily for us, we were blessed with twins—which seemed to make the decision that much easier!

Naming someone is a powerful act. Naming a person can allow us to recognize our gratitude for previous generations, remember a dear friend, or honor someone who has left a deep impression upon our lives. We often choose the name of someone we would want our child to imitate as they grow and develop over the years.

Today we are reminded that the angel asked that Mary's child be given the name Jesus, meaning "the one who saves." Paul tells us that it is through Jesus, the Son of God, that we are redeemed as God's children who bear Christ's name. When we attempt to imitate the life of Jesus, we are blessed with the presence of the Spirit, allowing us to intimately name God as "Abba, Father."

At the beginning of this year, we are blessed with many possibilities. We often make New Year's resolutions and strive to make these blessings last as we vow to improve our lives. The Church asks us to accept, as Mary did, the invitation to imitate Jesus more closely, to accept to be named a more sincere follower of Christ, and to receive the blessing of peace that accompanies this gift. **JOSEPH GUNN**

PEOPLE AND PRAYERS TO REMEMBER
THIS WEEK

Responding *to the* Word

Mary reflected in her heart about her experience with Jesus. ***How might I find more time for prayer during the coming year?***

READINGS
OF THE DAY

Numbers 6:22-27

Psalm 67

Galatians 4:4-7

Luke 2:16-21

Final Thoughts...

SUNDAY **JANUARY 3**

EPIPHANY *of the* **LORD**

Matthew is the only evangelist who tells the story of wise men from the East who follow a star in their search for the new-born King of the Jews. These "wise men" might be practitioners of Eastern mystical traditions, Babylonian astrologers, Arabian magicians, or rich adventure-seekers. They come from another world and are seeking something extraordinary. We can easily see in these travelers the restless searchers of our own age—people who keep looking for the ultimate experience, the perfect path, the next big thing.

We continue to tell and reflect upon their story as part of our own journey, more than 2,000 years later. The wise men are more than just "New Agers" from an ancient time. They follow the signs and they show us the star.

That star, pointing to the Christ child, is still part of our world today. Sometimes our work may be to polish the star and make it shine when it has been obscured by clouds of doubt, scandal, or suspicion. Sometimes we have the privilege of pointing it out to restless searchers; and sometimes we are the ones out in the dark, cold night, needing to get back up on the camel and follow the star again...until it leads us once more to the Christ-child who brings life and joy for the whole world. **MARILYN SWEET**

PEOPLE AND PRAYERS TO REMEMBER THIS WEEK

Responding *to the* Word

The magi followed a star to find Jesus.
Who or what has been like that star leading me to find Jesus in my life?

READINGS OF THE DAY

Isaiah 60:1-6

Psalm 72

Ephesians 3:2-3a, 5-6

Matthew 2:1-12

Final Thoughts...

FEASTS THIS WEEK

January 4: **St. Elizabeth Ann Seton**

January 5: **St. John Neumann**

January 6: **St. André Bessette**

January 7: **St. Raymond of Penyafort**

SUNDAY **JANUARY 10**

BAPTISM *of the* **LORD**

She was dressed in a lavender cashmere sweater. A single strand of pearls matching her earrings rested elegantly in its folds. Her hair was carefully coiffed, makeup freshly applied, perfume sweet and subtle. She smiled at her husband tenderly holding her hand. He smiled back at her, eyes questioning, seeking a flicker of recognition.

"She doesn't make connections much anymore," he whispered. "It's a terrible disease, Alzheimer's." He wiped away another tear that traced its way down his cheek.

Daily he dresses her, does her hair, and applies her makeup. He reads the papers to her and shares stories with her of their grandchildren's accomplishments and endless discoveries. He feeds her the breakfast that is delivered to her room at eight and ensures she eats the lunch that arrives at noon.

"You are my beloved Son; with you I am well pleased." Words spoken by the Father to the Son are words spoken by the Father to us on the day of our baptism. Each one held in divine tenderness; clothed in dignity; anointed with oil for service, witness, and belonging.

His care for her is more than simple duty. Grounded in vows long ago uttered in Christian faith, he sees beyond her Alzheimer's to the precious child of God she is, fully deserving of respect, affection, care, attention, and the preservation of dignity that God intends for all his children. **REV. ROGER KEELER**

PEOPLE AND PRAYERS TO REMEMBER THIS WEEK

READINGS OF THE DAY

Isaiah 55:1-11

Isaiah 12

1 John 5:1-9

Mark 1:7-11

Responding *to the* **Word**

Like Jesus at his baptism, we are also identified at our baptism as God's beloved child. ***What does being a child of God mean to me?***

Final Thoughts...

FEASTS THIS WEEK

January 13: **St. Hilary**

SUNDAY **JANUARY 17**

2ND SUNDAY *in* ORDINARY TIME

Week of Prayer for Christian Unity (January 18-25)

Do you remember, as a child, never being able to walk at your own pace and always running alongside a parent who was in a hurry? Now I do it to my own daughter. Hurry up, I say, we'll be late. And when I am working to a deadline, I don't welcome her interruptions. Even worse, I don't even hear them.

Jesus has a mission and an approaching deadline. Yet when he becomes aware of two young men following him, instead of ignoring them or hurrying ahead, he turns and asks them what they are looking for. Taken off guard, they reply awkwardly that they want to know where he lives. "Come and see," he replies.

To belong to this rabbi, they do not have to listen to a lecture denouncing other sects or learn a bunch of special rules or rituals. This rabbi turns to them, as soon as he is aware they are following him, and asks them what their heart truly desires. Then he invites them to get to know him, to spend time with him.

Each time we come to the Eucharist, we are answering Jesus' invitation to come and see. As Jesus invites us to come closer, do we know our own heart's desires? In following Jesus, may we join our neighbors with an open heart, journeying together to see where Jesus lives. **LOUISA BLAIR**

PEOPLE AND PRAYERS TO REMEMBER THIS WEEK

READINGS OF THE DAY

1 Samuel 3:3b-10, 19

Psalm 40

1 Corinthians 6:13c-15a, 17-20

John 1:35-42

Responding *to the* Word

The disciples search out Jesus but are not sure what they want from him. ***How would I answer if Jesus asked me, "What are you looking for?"***

Final Thoughts...

FEASTS THIS WEEK

January 20: **St. Fabian**
St. Sebastian

January 21: **St. Agnes**

January 22: **Day of Prayer for the Legal Protection of Unborn Children**

January 23: **St. Vincent**
St. Marianne Cope

SUNDAY **JANUARY 24**

3RD SUNDAY *in* ORDINARY TIME

Sunday of the Word of God

A lot of the decisions we make in life are leaps of faith. We can't be sure that moving away, starting a relationship, having a child, or changing careers will pan out in the long run, but when it feels right, we do it anyway.

The Second Vatican Council was such a leap of faith. One of the currents of fresh air to blow through the newly opened windows of the Church was the desire to build bridges to other Christian traditions, find common ground and restore unity. I have never known a time when Christian unity was discouraged. Born the year Vatican II began, I grew up immersed in this spirit of new possibilities.

During the Week of Prayer for Christian Unity, all Christians are invited to set aside their differences in order to celebrate their common faith in Jesus Christ. Across the country and around the world, they are gathering in each other's churches to pray and worship together this week, not knowing exactly where their actions will lead, but having faith that their gathering is important.

Have faith. In today's Scriptures we hear this invitation over and over again. The Ninevites believe and repent. The Psalmist trusts in God's goodness. Paul asks the Corinthians to look beyond this world. And Jesus asks some ordinary fishermen to abandon all that is familiar. Two thousand years later, these messages are still urgent. Can we also leave our nets—and our fears and our differences—and together follow Jesus? It's a leap of faith! **ANNE LOUISE MAHONEY**

PEOPLE AND PRAYERS TO REMEMBER THIS WEEK

READINGS OF THE DAY

Jonah 3:1-5, 10

Psalm 25

1 Corinthians 7:29-31

Mark 1:14-20

Responding *to the* Word

Jesus calls disciples to use their skills for building God's kingdom community. ***Which gift or skill do I bring to the building of this community?***

Final Thoughts...

FEASTS THIS WEEK

January 25: **Conversion of St. Paul**

January 26: **St. Timothy & St. Titus**

January 27: **St. Angela Merici**

January 28: **St. Thomas Aquinas**

SUNDAY **JANUARY 31**

4TH SUNDAY *in* ORDINARY TIME

When we think about authority, we often think of power that controls people. Governments, employers, and parents can use their authority to impose their wishes on citizens, employees, and children. This kind of authority succeeds by rules and laws and sometimes uses threats and coercion.

By contrast, the authority we hear about in today's readings is empowering. God promises Moses that he will put his words into the mouth of a prophet who will speak what God commands. Because this prophet will speak with God's authority, God's people will be accountable for their actions. God's voice has the power to change their hearts, and the people are responsible for heeding God's word.

In Mark's gospel we see the promise of this authority fulfilled in Jesus and realized in his loving words and actions. In the synagogue, the disciples recognize that Jesus is different from the scribes, who preach rules and laws. Both the disciples and the unclean spirit recognize this new and powerful authority. Rather than ruling by fear or intimidation, Jesus brings healing and wholeness, and reports of this new way of speaking God's word spread near and far.

As Christians we too are called to draw on this loving, life-giving authority. Today, by our baptism and our participation in the Eucharist, we are called to be disciples of God's love and care in our world. **SUSAN BERLINGERI**

Responding *to the* Word

Jesus' mastery of unclean spirits shows he is reordering the world for God. ***How has my life been reordered because of my faith in Christ?***

PEOPLE AND PRAYERS TO REMEMBER
THIS WEEK

READINGS
OF THE DAY

Deuteronomy 18:15-20

Psalm 95

1 Corinthians 7:32-35

Mark 1:21-28

Final Thoughts...

FEASTS THIS WEEK

February 2: **Presentation of the Lord**

February 3: **St. Blaise**
St. Ansgar

February 5: **St. Agatha**

February 6: **St. Paul Miki & Companions**

SUNDAY **FEBRUARY 7**

5TH SUNDAY *in* ORDINARY TIME

We sometimes say, "There's no rest for the wicked." For Job, troubled and even angry with God, there seems to be no rest even for the just. Despite his anger at God, however, Job remains in his heart a person of faith and prayer.

Paul endured suffering as well. For the sake of the gospel, he became the servant of all, forfeiting everything so that no obstacle might stand between the gospel and those to whom he proclaimed it. The blessings the gospel brings were reward enough for him.

By contrast, the crowds in today's gospel hunt Jesus down, seeing not who he is beyond the cures. Unlike Simon's mother-in-law, they do not yet understand the service to others that is required of those who have been saved by Christ. Jesus does not leave them behind out of coldness on his part; he does so in order to proclaim the real message of salvation, which is not about incidental healings but about a Messiah who will win salvation for all through his suffering and death.

In the face of human misery, the very best words of comfort do not explain suffering away but proclaim the good news that Christ bore our sickness and endured our suffering. Not watching our suffering from afar, Christ has been and is with us, offering healing to the broken-hearted through a share in his resurrection. For this, we offer grateful praise. **CHRISTINE MADER**

PEOPLE AND PRAYERS TO REMEMBER THIS WEEK

Responding *to the* **Word**

Job recognizes the difficulties of life and how they push us to give up hope. ***How does Christ's presence in my life offer hope?***

READINGS OF THE DAY

Job 7:1-4, 6-7

Psalm 147

1 Corinthians 9:16-19, 22-23

Mark 1:29-39

Final Thoughts...

FEASTS THIS WEEK

February 8: **St. Jerome Emiliani**
St. Josephine Bakhita

February 10: **Ash Wednesday**

February 11: **Our Lady of Lourdes**

WEDNESDAY **FEBRUARY 10**

ASH WEDNESDAY

Driving home from work the other day I spotted some food for thought on a sign posted in front of a local soup kitchen: "If you want to know your values, look at what you've done today."

I pondered. I belong to Amnesty International. I've volunteered at this very soup kitchen. I discuss these experiences with others so they will be influenced to do the same. I work for social justice.

I fell short of this task when I looked at what I had done that day: Amnesty International's last two letter-writing campaigns lay unread under a pile of papers somewhere on my desk; and it has been over two years since I had found time to go back to volunteer at the soup kitchen.

My list of what I'd done today was an eye-opener. I had used past actions to make myself appear greater in my own eyes and the eyes of others. Without daily application, my values had gone up in smoke. My values without actions were lifeless. I resolved that out of the ashes of my false identity I would recommit myself to expressing my values quietly in my everyday life.

Now, where are those letter-writing campaigns...and what's the number of the soup kitchen? **JOHN WEIR**

Responding *to the* Word

Joel wants us to change on the inside and not just externally. ***What change of attitude do I most want to make this Lent?***

PEOPLE AND PRAYERS TO REMEMBER
THIS WEEK

READINGS
OF THE DAY

Joel 2:12-18

Psalm 51

2 Corinthians 5:20–6:2

Matthew 6:1-6, 16-18

Final Thoughts...

SUNDAY **FEBRUARY 14**

1ST SUNDAY *of* LENT

Mark's gospel is stark, direct, pared to essentials—appropriate somehow as Lent begins. His words reflect the Lenten call to return to basics in our relationship with God. And they invite honest self-examination. The Spirit invites us to slow down and come away into the quiet of the wilderness to restore our souls. As individuals and as Church, we are called to enter the desert and renew our commitment to proclaiming the good news.

The desert is an empty and arid place associated with loneliness and struggle. It is also a metaphor for our inward journey of self-awareness, as we look honestly at ourselves and our temptations, our misplaced desires and loyalties. The desert can become a place of spiritual honing, of growth in love, but we must do as Jesus did—we must obey the Spirit's invitation and prepare for the journey inward.

It takes courage to enter the desert, to surrender to the probing and prompting of the Spirit. "Repent and believe" involves refocusing. Are we open to what the Spirit has to say to us this Lent about our temptations? Our areas of darkness? Our pain? Our brokenness? Our potential for transformation? Will we listen for the Spirit's wisdom and grow in our ability to build the kingdom? Will we become more fully the face of Christ, of love, in our world?

Lent and the desert are both stations on our way, helping us learn to proclaim the good news whatever the cost. **ELLA ALLEN**

PEOPLE AND PRAYERS TO REMEMBER THIS WEEK

READINGS OF THE DAY

Genesis 9:8-15

Psalm 25

1 Peter 3:18-22

Mark 1:12-15

Responding *to the* Word

Jesus' desert experience led to a new ministry for others. ***Is there a desert experience in my life which has invited me to be more of service to others?***

Final Thoughts...

FEASTS THIS WEEK

February 17: **The Seven Holy Founders of the Servite Order**

SUNDAY **FEBRUARY 21**

2ND SUNDAY *of* LENT

Today's powerful readings tell stories of extraordinary love between father and son. Tested to the limit, Abraham's trust in God is so great that he is ready to make an unthinkable sacrifice. Most people look at this and wonder why an all-loving God would put anyone to such a test. It is only when we read the gospel that we see the parallel between the two stories of loving fathers.

The lesson we learn in the story of Abraham is complete trust in God. It is fortunate that in our faith journey our trust is not often put to such a test. However, no one gets through life without some difficulties; we all have our faith tested from time to time. The death of a loved one; the loss of a seemingly secure job; the inability to prevent war and conflict, hunger and disease—these are all tests of our faith in God and in one another.

We can use this season of Lent as our personal time of reflection, knowing that God is with us as we seek solutions for all our problems. We can look back on our lives and be aware that God has always walked with us. We can examine our present difficulty and know that God is again at our side. And we can be assured that in the future God will never be far away. **CHRISTINA ROGERS**

PEOPLE AND PRAYERS TO REMEMBER
THIS WEEK

READINGS
OF THE DAY

Genesis 22:1-2, 9a, 10-13, 15-18

Psalm 116

Romans 8:31b-34

Mark 9:2-10

Responding *to the* **Word**

Abraham was asked to sacrifice what was most dear to him—his beloved son. ***What might I need to give up to live more closely with God?***

Final Thoughts...

FEASTS THIS WEEK

February 22: **Chair of St. Peter**

February 23: **St. Polycarp**

February 27: **St. Gregory of Narek**

SUNDAY **FEBRUARY 28**

3RD SUNDAY *of* LENT

Spring is a time for sprucing up. After a long winter, many of us enjoy being outdoors in the fresh air, cleaning the yard or preparing the soil for the garden. Our home and its surroundings are put in order and made beautiful.

Lent is a time when we do a spring cleaning of our souls. We take an inventory of our lives by asking ourselves how we are living and where we need to change. What kind of debris lies between our relationship with God and our concern for others? This is the time when we pull up the weeds of self-centeredness, laziness, and rash judgments about others. The tools we use in cleansing our hearts are prayer and reflection with the Scriptures, fasting for justice in the world, and sharing our resources with others in need. The gospel story of Jesus ridding the Temple of the profit-driven merchants is a constant reminder and invitation to us that now is the time to rid our hearts of all that is not from God.

We participate in the sacrament of the Eucharist so that we may be nourished by God's love and have the zeal to embrace the mystery of the cross already planted in the garden of our hearts. Soon we will breathe the fresh air of the resurrection.

REV. ROBERT F. DUEWEKE, O.S.A.

PEOPLE AND PRAYERS TO REMEMBER THIS WEEK

READINGS OF THE DAY

Exodus 20:1-17

Psalm 19

1 Corinthians 1:22-25

John 2:13-25

Responding *to the* Word

God's commandments reveal the way for us to have a good community.

Which commandment is hardest for me to observe now in my life?

Final Thoughts...

FEASTS THIS WEEK

March 3: **St. Katharine Drexel**

March 4: **St. Casimir**

SUNDAY **MARCH 7**

4TH SUNDAY *of* LENT

Have you ever been in love, head-over-heels in love? When we are, we want to give everything we have to our lover. But imagine how devastating it would be to have our love rejected. That's what today's gospel is about—a love story.

For God so loved the world that he gave his only son. Jesus died on the cross for our sins. Imagine how intense love must be to inspire a sacrifice like that. This sacrifice saved the world, saved all of us, and guaranteed an eternity in paradise. It would be hard to imagine anyone rejecting this love, hard to imagine anyone turning his or her back, not only on love, but also on the gift of eternal life.

But that is what we do when we sin. We reject God's love. And in that rejection we walk away from everything—from love, from life, from eternal paradise. That's the meaning of the sacrifice on the cross. When Jesus died for our sins we were saved. With every drop of his precious blood we were promised eternal life. All we need do is accept the gift, accept God's love.

It all sounds pretty simple. But we all know life isn't always so simple. We get distracted. We mean to do the right thing but temptations get in the way. We slip and we fall. God understands. God has already forgiven us. All we need to do is turn toward God and accept God's love. Imagine that! **PATRICK M. DOYLE**

Responding *to the* Word

God sends messengers to invite the people to change their ways. ***Who is God sending me to help me make my Lenten changes?***

PEOPLE AND PRAYERS TO REMEMBER THIS WEEK

READINGS OF THE DAY

2 Chronicles 36:14-16, 19-23

Psalm 137

Ephesians 2:4-10

John 3:14-21

Final Thoughts...

FEASTS THIS WEEK

March 8: **St. John of God**

March 9: **St. Frances of Rome**

SUNDAY **MARCH 14**

5TH SUNDAY *of* LENT

There are times (perhaps you share this) when I read the gospels and think: what would it feel like to be part of that crowd listening to Jesus? Imagine being there when Jesus tells a story or gestures in your direction! Would I understand the profound nature of what Jesus is saying, or would I miss the point entirely? Fortunately, I have the benefit of the entire gospels and the luxury of time to reflect.

The grain of wheat dying and bearing much fruit is one of my favorite examples. The whole purpose of Jesus' death (and resurrection) was to make a positive change in the way people relate to God, to one another, and to creation. Has this event made a difference in our lives? How much fruit has resulted from the death of this single grain?

Each act of kindness, toward a loved one or a stranger, is a step in the right direction. Every time a government enacts a policy that focuses on the well-being of communities and individuals, it moves us forward on the right path. And even the smallest act of solidarity and support that we show for people around the world who are working for justice and liberation is another move forward.

As our Lenten journey nears its conclusion, may we profit from the gospels and our reflection, to "get the message" and work for a bountiful harvest. **SUSAN EATON**

PEOPLE AND PRAYERS TO REMEMBER
THIS WEEK

READINGS
OF THE DAY

Jeremiah 31:31-34

Psalm 51

Hebrews 5:7-9

John 12:20-33

Responding *to the* Word

Jeremiah foresees a time when God's law will be written on our hearts.

What new experience of God's loving guidance have I felt this Lent?

Final Thoughts...

FEASTS THIS WEEK

March 17: **St. Patrick**

March 18: **St. Cyril of Jerusalem**

March 19: **St. Joseph**

SUNDAY **MARCH 21**

PALM SUNDAY *of the* **PASSION** *of the* **LORD**

We see reflected in today's gospel many faces of passion. All these faces have something to teach us.

First there is the wordless passion of a nameless woman who poured out her love for Jesus and anointed him for death. Side by side with this there is Judas' silent kiss of betrayal. Wordless passion can either bless or crucify.

Soldiers and guards taunt a defenseless Jesus. The crowd allows themselves to be led like sheep, shouting "Crucify him!" Cowardly passion has grave consequences.

Peter displays great passion. The all too familiar bravado—"Even though all should have their faith shaken, mine will not be"—followed quickly by betrayal and bitter tears. In the end Peter's passion is a passion redeemed. Peter's experience speaks of the unconditional love of God.

Jesus' passion is the consuming passion of a man wishing to leave a living remembrance of a life well spent—the quiet passion of a man who faces terrible derision and ridicule with utmost calm—the passion of a man who begs his Father to take this cup away and cries out in utter despair on the cross, feeling entirely forsaken. Jesus' passion changed the face of our world forever.

How do I live my daily passion? How does my passion, be it wordless, cowardly, redeemed, or pure, change my world and those closest to me? Passion can be either death-dealing or life-giving. Which is it in my life? **KAREN JOHNSON**

Responding *to the* Word

Isaiah describes God's faithful servant who suffers but is later rewarded. ***What has been the hardest aspect of my Lenten time?***

PEOPLE AND PRAYERS TO REMEMBER
THIS WEEK

READINGS
OF THE DAY

Mark 11:1-10 *or*
John 12:12-16
(Procession)

Isaiah 50:4-7

Psalm 22

Philippians 2:6-11

Mark 14:1–15:47

Final Thoughts...

THURSDAY **MARCH 25**

MASS *of the* **LORD'S SUPPER (HOLY THURSDAY)**

In the gospel today, Jesus says "I have given you a model to follow, so that as I have done for you, you should also do.." But what is the lesson? Are we literally to wash one another's feet? I think not. In the ancient world, roads were not paved and walking was the primary form of transport. Given the dust and mud, feet got very dirty. The first thing a person did on coming to a house was wash his feet, a job often done by a servant. Here, at the final supper, the host and master takes the lesser role of a servant to the disciples. By his example, Jesus shows that love does not seek prestige and status. It lives in the lowly acts of service freely given to others.

Perhaps Jesus knew that the disciples who were with him on the final night of his life might be tempted to use their special position to "lord it over others" later. Luke tells us that the disciples had been arguing over who was the greatest among them. So, they needed a lesson, an unforgettable reminder, that following Jesus means serving others.

We come to the Eucharist to receive Christ. By receiving him, we take on his life. To take on his life is to take on his love-made-concrete in service to others, too. The incarnation and resurrection are God's love made flesh. And so we incarnate that love as we serve others and give away the love we have received. **REV. JAMES B. SAUER**

Responding *to the* Word

At the Passover, the Jews remembered God's powerful presence that transformed their oppression into freedom.
How has God freed me from some oppression this Lent?

PEOPLE AND PRAYERS TO REMEMBER THIS WEEK

READINGS OF THE DAY

Exodus 12:1-8, 11-14

Psalm 116

1 Corinthians 11:23-26

John 13:1-15

Final Thoughts...

FRIDAY **MARCH 26**

CELEBRATION *of the* **PASSION** *of the* **LORD (GOOD FRIDAY)**

Good Friday is the only day of the year when the Church does not celebrate the Eucharist. There are no flowers, no candles, no music. Even the altar is bare. Today's liturgy moves us into the bleak reality of human suffering and death. All is focused on the cross, on Jesus' passion and death.

The first reading speaks of innocent suffering, the violent death of one whose life was given completely to others. It raises the perennial question of why the innocent suffer, giving no answers, but making it clear that suffering is not God's punishment for wrongdoing. Neither the Suffering Servant of Isaiah nor Jesus have done anything to warrant their suffering.

In the gospel we see Jesus surrounded by people, yet alone in his suffering. Peter denies knowing him. In this version of the Passion narrative, John tells us that Jesus carried the cross alone, with no one to help. Jesus knew what it was like to be alone in his suffering and death.

Today we are left to contemplate and stay with the darkness, knowing that, at one time or another, this is our own experience. Like Jesus we feel isolated in our pain, and with Jesus we know there is no denying its reality. Yet today's liturgy reminds us that for all our feelings of isolation, we are never truly alone. Jesus himself knew the depths of human suffering. **SR. BARBARA BOZAK, C.S.J.**

PEOPLE AND PRAYERS TO REMEMBER THIS WEEK

READINGS OF THE DAY

Isaiah 52:13–53:12

Psalm 31

Hebrews 4:14-16; 5:7-9

John 18:1–19:42

Responding *to the* Word

Jesus shares our human weakness but never lets that create a separation from God. ***What weakness or suffering has tempted me to question God's love for me?***

Final Thoughts...

SATURDAY **MARCH 27**

RESURRECTION *of the* **LORD (EASTER VIGIL)**

My husband and I have had the privilege of proclaiming the first reading at the Easter Vigil service in our parish. In reading it aloud, I find myself deeply moved by the poetry of the Genesis creation story. I am particularly struck by the affirming refrain, "God saw how good it was."

Interwoven with my sense of awe and gratitude, however, is a thread of sadness and shame. For it seems that every day the news media remind us of the damage we humans are doing to God's beautiful creation by polluting our air and water and soil. We are selfishly desecrating what God has made to be so good.

Fast forward to tonight's gospel passage: the women go to the tomb, wondering who will roll back the stone from the entrance. Once they arrive they find the stone moved, and inside they find a young man sitting, clothed in a white robe. Are they filled with joy at the discovery? Mark tells us "they were utterly amazed."

The women move from questioning to being "utterly amazed." What are we to make of these contrasting colors woven into the fabric of this "most blessed of all nights"? They remind us that we cannot authentically celebrate Christ's victory over sin and death without at the same time acknowledging our own weakness and our utter dependence on God.

The reign of God is very much a work-in-progress; we are called to be humble and faithful co-creators with God in bringing that work to fruition. **KRYSTYNA HIGGINS**

PEOPLE AND PRAYERS TO REMEMBER THIS WEEK

READINGS OF THE DAY

Genesis 1:1–2:2

Psalm 104 *or* **Psalm 33**

Genesis 22:1-18

Psalm 16

Exodus 14:15–15:1

Exodus 15

Isaiah 54:5-14

Psalm 30

Isaiah 55:1-11

Isaiah 12

Baruch 3:9-15, 32–4:4

Psalm 19

Ezekiel 36:16-17a, 18-28

Psalm 42 *or* **Psalm 51**

Romans 6:3-11

Psalm 118

Mark 16:1-7

Responding *to the* Word

Paul reminds us that through our relationship with Jesus we are drawn into the mystery of life and death and new life. ***What hint of new life is beginning in me at this Easter time?***

Final Thoughts...

SUNDAY **MARCH 28**

RESURRECTION *of the* LORD (EASTER SUNDAY)

The death and resurrection of Jesus Christ is the great sign of God's passion to restore humanity and all creation to its original blessing. Celebrating Holy Week and Easter enables us to enter again into the wonder and mystery of what our God has done for us. Here we rediscover the amazing truth of a peaceful God who seeks only to embrace humanity in all our frailties, to forgive our sins, and to invite us to become transformed into the One who is Risen.

Our Easter gospel features two special people and the empty tomb of the Risen Christ. The beloved disciple, with a heart transformed by the sacred events of Jesus' passion and death, upon entering the empty tomb immediately saw and believed. Mary Magdalene, while tearfully, earnestly, seeking the sacred body, instead finds a young man clothed in a white robe, who tells her that Jesus "has been raised." Persevering hope is transformed by the gift and joy of encounter. What great news she has to tell the others.

Distracted by the busyness in our lives, we are often unaware that the Risen Christ seeks to encounter us daily. But when we look at our reality with hearts hungry for this encounter, God will surprise us: in the joy on children's faces, a gesture of reassurance in anguished moment, a blessing of forgiveness, an unexpected sense of the holy in our daily dying and rising. This is what makes us an Easter people. We can witness both in joy and pain to an unshakable hope that comes from knowing the Risen Christ who has overcome all for our sake, and for the world. **REV. MICHAEL TRAHER, S.F.M.**

PEOPLE AND PRAYERS TO REMEMBER THIS WEEK

READINGS OF THE DAY

Acts 10:34a, 37-43

Psalm 118

Colossians 3:1-4 *or* **1 Corinthians 5:6b-8**

John 20:1-9 *or* **Mark 16:1-7** *(Vigil)* *or* **Luke 24:13-35** *(afternoon)*

Responding *to the* Word

Peter's speech summarizes the Christian motive for mission: when we experience the risen Christ, we proclaim this message to others. ***How might I share my belief in Jesus' resurrection with others today?***

Final Thoughts...

SUNDAY **APRIL 4**

2ND SUNDAY *of* EASTER

Divine Mercy Sunday

Thomas did something we would all like to do. It would be so much easier to believe if we could touch and see the wounds of Christ. Yet the wounds of Christ are present every day in many different ways. I can still touch them; perhaps I just fail to see them.

We are all wounded. Some of us carry wounds that are deeper and more intense than others. These wounds can be physical or spiritual, recent or long-standing. An injection or a pill isn't enough to heal these wounds. Healing is an internal process that puts things right, and to do this we need to face our wounds.

Jesus carries our wounds. In today's gospel, not only is Jesus inviting Thomas to feel the wounds in his hands and side; Jesus also invites Thomas to face Thomas' own wounds which Jesus is carrying. It is only by facing his wounds that Thomas can be healed and then say, "My Lord and my God!"

Today, we like Thomas are being invited to face our wounds which Jesus carries for us. Like Thomas, we are being invited to heal whatever it is that threatens life within us.

In this Eucharist today, may we find the strength to say "My Lord and my God!" and allow the grace Jesus offers to heal the wounds that prevent us from being whole. **ANTHONY CHEZZI**

PEOPLE AND PRAYERS TO REMEMBER THIS WEEK

Responding *to the* Word

The earliest Christian community was distinguished by its sharing of goods. ***What sharing of my goods might I undertake this week?***

READINGS OF THE DAY

Acts 4:32-35

Psalm 118

1 John 5:1-6

John 20:19-31

Final Thoughts...

FEASTS THIS WEEK

April 5: **Annunciation of the Lord**
April 7: **St. John Baptist de la Salle**

SUNDAY **APRIL 11**

3RD SUNDAY *of* EASTER

When has God's presence been made known to you? Did it arise in a surprising way? The two disciples who encountered Jesus on the road to Emmaus didn't recognize him at first. After all, they only recognized Jesus at the breaking of the bread. In today's gospel, Jesus also ate broiled fish with the befuddled disciples, and then he opened their minds to understand the Scriptures.

Meals can often be special moments of life-giving encounter. When we pause in our too-busy lives and stop to listen and feel what is being said, we can often encounter a moment of grace. Has there been, in your own life, a special meal with friends or family when you have keenly felt the presence of the Other?

Just such a special moment happened for me in a Tim Horton's restaurant in Halifax. There, a good friend I hadn't seen in years recounted how he had made sense of his incredible experiences as a missionary in Latin America. I longed for the coffee never to grow cold, for the cup never to be emptied, so we could continue to go deeper in our reflections and sharing.

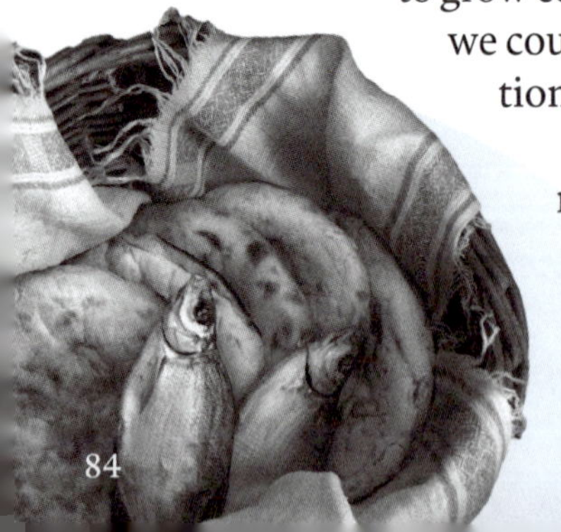

We need more such "Emmaus moments" in our lives—times when God is so very close that we can feel the Loving Presence in a deep way—and then fully respond. **JOSEPH GUNN**

Responding *to the* Word

Peter encourages repentance—changing our lives to relate in a new way to God. ***How can I continue the changes I began during Lent and grow in my relationship to God and others?***

PEOPLE AND PRAYERS TO REMEMBER THIS WEEK

READINGS OF THE DAY

Acts 3:13-15, 17-19

Psalm 4

1 John 2:1-5a

Luke 24:35-48

Final Thoughts...

FEASTS THIS WEEK

April 13: **St. Martin I**

SUNDAY **APRIL 18**

4TH SUNDAY *of* EASTER

World Day of Prayer for Vocations

Some commercials can give the impression that "the good life" means to eat, drink, drive, and wear certain brand products. So we in the Church need to affirm again and again the rejected cornerstone, Jesus, who reveals the sacred dignity of human life.

Today is Vocation Sunday. From the Latin *vocare*, vocation means to call. Vocation means that we, God's beloved, are called to grow in love for God and neighbor. No matter what our job or role, we are all called into a lifetime pilgrimage of becoming fully human, fully alive with the love of God.

Today, we hear the words of the good shepherd gospel. The same Eternal Word that became flesh in Jesus longs to become flesh in our lives—in our home, workplace, parish, global marketplace. Indeed, there is no shortage of need for compassionate people who continue Jesus' mission.

Good shepherds dream of a better, more human world. They promote justice. They seek peace. Committed to the common good, they tenderly care for those in anguish. For the sake of love, they courageously stand their ground in lonely places, not running from threatening wolves. Aware of their own weakness, they find strength in the Eucharist. Good shepherds preach the gospel not so much with words as by the genuine love and integrity of their actions. Easy to say. Humbling to live. Yet, day-by-day we are invited to humbly open our hearts to God's love. To become good shepherds befits the dignity of our humanity. **STEVE HILL**

PEOPLE AND PRAYERS TO REMEMBER THIS WEEK

Responding *to the* Word

Jesus tells us he knows our uniqueness just like a shepherd knows his sheep. ***How does it change me to know that Jesus loves me the way I am so he can help me be the way God wants me to be?***

READINGS OF THE DAY

Acts 4:8-12

Psalm 118

1 John 3:1-2

John 10:11-18

Final Thoughts...

FEASTS THIS WEEK

April 21: **St. Anselm**

April 23: **St. George**
St. Adalbert

April 24: **St. Fidelis of Sigmaringen**

SUNDAY **APRIL 25**

5TH SUNDAY *of* EASTER

Vineyards were never a part of my experience as I was growing up. Maybe that's why I could never relate to the image of Jesus as the true vine.

Then I had the opportunity to live in a wine-growing area. I saw the process up-close from beginning to end. Then I understood! I came in autumn and saw the full harvest first. There were thick bunches of plump, juicy grapes suspended from lush vines that extended out as far as I could see. After the grapes were collected the branches were cut down and burned. The fields strewn with stumps appeared too barren to ever produce again. They rested all winter until, come spring, tiny buds emerged and the process began again. The vine, rooted in rich soil, held the promise of life, the kind of life Jesus describes in the gospel.

Jesus is the vine—he remains the same yesterday, today, and forever. We are the branches—we come and go on this earth. The fruit we bear is offered to a hungry and thirsty world. We participate in the mission of Jesus and when our mission is fulfilled, we let go and yield to those who follow us.

As we come together at Eucharist we draw our sustenance from the Vine. We pray together the prayer of the One who invites us to the banquet: "Take this, all of you, and drink from it."

SR. MARY ELLEN GREEN, O.P.

PEOPLE AND PRAYERS TO REMEMBER THIS WEEK

Responding *to the* Word

Jesus tells us that we can only survive if we join ourselves to his life. ***What can I do this week to invite Jesus to "remain in me"?***

READINGS OF THE DAY

Acts 9:26-31

Psalm 22

1 John 3:18-24

John 15:1-8

Final Thoughts...

FEASTS THIS WEEK

April 28: **St. Peter Chanel**
St. Louis Grignion de Montfort

April 29: **St. Catherine of Siena**

April 30: **St. Pius V**

May 1: **St. Joseph the Worker**

SUNDAY **MAY 2**

6TH SUNDAY *of* EASTER

In today's gospel Jesus uses the words "command" and "commandment" five times, urging his followers—including us—to obey his commandments.

"Command" is not a word that inspires a great response. It brings to mind thoughts of power and control, of being told what to do, of not being free. In our society, where the operating assumption is that we are all equal, being given a command makes us bristle. It makes us feel that we are not being treated as responsible adults. Yet even our children don't like being told what to do. How many parents have heard, "You're not the boss of me!" when they ask their children to do something?

When someone says to us, "I want you to obey my commands," we naturally expect to be given a list of things to do and not do. But, as he often does, Jesus confuses our expectations. He says that obeying his commands is a mark of friendship, not servitude; that obeying his commands is something that causes joy, not resentment; that his command is not a series of restrictions or regulations to be mindlessly followed, but one guiding principle that requires deep thought and reflection before being obeyed.

Jesus may be asking us to follow his commandments, but his challenge can be met only by those wise enough to understand what true obedience means. **PATRICK GALLAGHER**

PEOPLE AND PRAYERS TO REMEMBER THIS WEEK

READINGS OF THE DAY

Acts 10:25-26, 34-35, 44-48

Psalm 98

1 John 4:7-10

John 15:9-17

Responding *to the* **Word**

John summarizes God's whole existence as love—the power uniting persons to one another into a new community. ***How might I imitate God's love by relating more deeply to others?***

Final Thoughts...

FEASTS THIS WEEK

May 3: **St. Philip & St. James**

May 6: **Ascension of the Lord**
(in some dioceses of the USA)

SUNDAY **MAY 9**

THE ASCENSION *of the* **LORD**

World Communications Day

When we love another person, we are usually keen to show that love in concrete and selfless acts. In fact, the authenticity of our love for someone is often measured by how much we are willing to turn away from ourselves and toward the other, in these acts of kindness and charity.

After the resurrection, the disciples meet Jesus in his new life. In the resurrected and ascended Lord, humanity, once an image and likeness of God but distorted by sin, has been restored to its ultimate place in the presence of God. Now, at each meeting with the disciples, the risen Lord communicates that divine loving presence.

Having grown in God's saving love, the disciples turn away from themselves and toward the needs of their brothers and sisters, proclaiming the saving power of God to "every creature." They are sent to stare down the demons of selfishness and greed, and to protect the people from the poisons of hatred and disunity.

In today's liturgy let us open our hearts to the love of the risen Lord so that we, too, may hear his voice sending us forth to love and serve "every creature." In our effort to become faithful communicators of the message of salvation, let us remember that the measure of authenticity of our encounter with the love of the risen Lord consists in our acts of charity and kindness. **ANTAL PROKECZ**

** The 7th Sunday of Easter is celebrated in some dioceses of the USA today. Refer to page 99.*

PEOPLE AND PRAYERS TO REMEMBER THIS WEEK

Responding *to the* Word

After his Ascension, Jesus continued to work through the disciples. ***When have I most felt that God was working through me?***

READINGS OF THE DAY

Acts 1:1-11

Psalm 47

Ephesians 1:17-23
***or* Ephesians 4:1-13**

Mark 16:15-20

Final Thoughts...

FEASTS THIS WEEK

May 10: **St. John De Avila**
St. Damien de Veuster

May 12: **St. Nereus & St. Achilleus**
St. Pancras

May 13: **Our Lady of Fatima**

May 14: **St. Matthias**

May 15: **St. Isidore**

SUNDAY **MAY 9**

7TH SUNDAY *of* EASTER

But now I am coming to you.
I speak this in the world so that they may share my joy completely. **[JOHN 17.13]**

We are reminded of Jesus' sacrifices in today's gospel; he was human and did walk among us. All that we have been blessed with and are grateful for is because of Jesus' fulfillment of Scripture. Although the concept of this sacrifice is presented to us during each Eucharist, this Sunday offers a unique opportunity to reflect on the words of Christ prior to the crucifixion. With them comes a flood of emotion, as we truly grasp the idea that we give ourselves to God in a similar spiritual fashion. The gospel teaches us that although no one has seen God, his love completes us as individuals and presents itself to others.

This Easter season has been an opportunity for each of us to demonstrate the love and appreciation we have for one another, since we're taught to embody and exemplify God's love for us. Take the time to lend a helping hand, to remind a loved one that they are in fact loved and cherished, and to embrace the ultimate form of love through the acknowledgment that "God is love, and whoever remains in love remains in God and God in him." **MATTHEW SOTTILE**

PEOPLE AND PRAYERS TO REMEMBER THIS WEEK

Responding *to the* Word

Jesus prays that we continue his work and stay free of evil. ***What can I do to be more attentive to the way evil can change my relation to God and others?***

READINGS OF THE DAY

Acts 1:15-17, 20a, 20c-26

Psalm 103

1 John 4:11-16

John 17:11b-19

Final Thoughts...

SUNDAY **MAY 16**

PENTECOST SUNDAY

The feast of Pentecost stirs anew our hearts as Christians. We are celebrating the humble beginnings of the Church. Empowered by the Holy Spirit, the first community of Jesus' disciples became prophetic, world-changing signs and witnesses for the kingdom of God, "to the ends of the earth."

Jesus taught clearly that sharing his mission to reveal God's kingdom is experienced and lived out through personal relationship with him. He called the disciples his friends and promised to be with them in the Holy Spirit—he would send them the Spirit of Truth to be their guide and companion.

As disciples of Jesus today, guided by the Spirit, we too are gifted with that same awesome relationship. Our unique witness is needed in the world to awaken and nurture the seeds of the kingdom sown by God in every human heart. But ever conscious of our human weakness, Paul today offers us a reality check: avoid behaviors and attitudes that do not contribute to the life of the kingdom. He reminds us instead to embrace the fruits of the Spirit which nurture us for living our mission: "love, joy, peace, patience, kindness, generosity, faithfulness, gentleness, and self-control."

This Pentecost, let us celebrate together the gifts of the Spirit that renew us in joy and courage for service of the kingdom of God. **REV. MICHAEL TRAHER, S.F.M.**

PEOPLE AND PRAYERS TO REMEMBER THIS WEEK

READINGS OF THE DAY

Acts 2:1-11

Psalm 104

1 Corinthians 12:3b-7, 12-13 *or* **Galatians 5:16-25**

John 20:19-23 *or* **John 15:26-27; 16:12-15**

Responding *to the* **Word**

The presence and power of God's Holy Spirit enabled the disciples to speak about Jesus. ***When have I felt the Spirit's prompting to share my love for Jesus with others?***

Final Thoughts...

FEASTS THIS WEEK

May 17: **Blessed Virgin Mary, Mother of the Church**

May 18: **St. John I**

May 20: **St. Bernardine of Siena**

May 21: **St. Christopher Magallanes & Companions**

May 22: **St. Rita of Cascia**

SUNDAY **MAY 23**

THE MOST HOLY TRINITY

God called and chose a people. As Moses says, God took "a nation for himself." This call was not about following rules but about relationship. God offers a covenant, not a contract. We are given rules, but they are to help us to live out that intimate relationship.

Jesus sent his disciples out to make more disciples. They were not simply finding people who would "observe all that I have commanded you," but people who would share in the relationship the disciples had with Christ, with the Father and with the Spirit. Paul tells us that the Holy Spirit is the key to our relationship with the Trinity. The Spirit, the bond between the Father and the Son, is alive in our midst, uniting us to the Trinity of love and to one another. The rules follow from and feed the relationship. It is relationship to which we are called.

God, mysteriously, lives in relationship: the Trinity, though one God, is a loving, life-giving relationship of three Divine Persons, and we are invited to share in that unity. Through the power of the Holy Spirit we can cry "Abba! Father," because we are co-heirs with Jesus our brother and children of his Father. We are people of great dignity and of great responsibility. We are the people the Lord has chosen as his heritage. **DINAH SIMMONS**

PEOPLE AND PRAYERS TO REMEMBER THIS WEEK

Responding *to the* Word

Moses reviews the story of God's mighty deeds done for the covenant people. ***What mighty deeds of God's loving power have been at work in my life?***

READINGS OF THE DAY

Deuteronomy 4:32-34, 39-40

Psalm 33

Romans 8:14-17

Matthew 28:16-20

Final Thoughts...

FEASTS THIS WEEK

May 25: **St. Bede the Venerable**
St. Gregory VII
St. Mary Magdalene de' Pazzi

May 26: **St. Philip Neri**

May 27: **St. Augustine of Canterbury**

May 29: **St. Paul VI**

THE MOST HOLY BODY *and* BLOOD *of* CHRIST

Think for a moment what it means that blood is in us to give. Whether donating to a blood bank, sacrificing ourselves for a worthy cause, or giving birth to our own children, are we not really talking about more than red and white corpuscles, platelets, and plasma? Do we not mean that life itself is in us to give?

The people of Israel chose blood to symbolize the pouring out of their lives to the God who had chosen them, redeemed them from slavery in Egypt, and made a covenant with them. Moses sprinkled both the altar (which stood for God) and the people with blood to show how intimate the bond between God and chosen people was.

Ideally, the story might have ended there. Instead, Israel's experience was an up-and-down one: the same people who had promised to be faithful would later build the golden calf. On the annual Day of Atonement, the high priest asked forgiveness for the people's sins when he entered the Holy of Holies (the Temple's innermost sanctuary) and sprinkled sacrificial blood on the mercy seat of God.

Although of value, the ritual had to be repeated. But Christ's sacrifice is once-for-all and cleanses us not only externally but in the depths of our hearts. Christ gave his very life for us and because of his love and forgiveness poured out, we now share in the divine life. In thanksgiving (Eucharist), let us give our own life's blood in loving service to others. **CHRISTINE MADER**

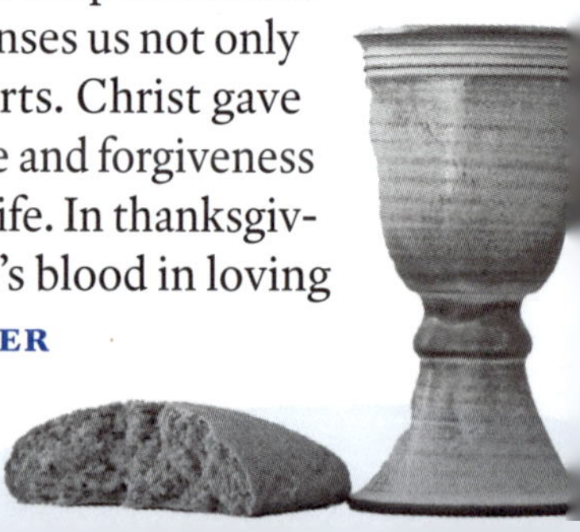

PEOPLE AND PRAYERS TO REMEMBER THIS WEEK

Responding *to the* Word

Jesus is the mediator between ourselves and God to deliver us from our sins. ***How can I express more gratitude for my gift of salvation?***

READINGS OF THE DAY

Exodus 24:3-8

Psalm 116

Hebrews 9:11-15

Mark 14:12-16, 22-26

Final Thoughts...

FEASTS THIS WEEK

May 31: **Visitation of the Blessed Virgin Mary**

June 1: **St. Justin**

June 2: **St. Marcellinus & St. Peter**

June 3: **St. Charles Lwanga & Companions**

June 4: **Most Sacred Heart of Jesus**

June 5: **Immaculate Heart of Mary**
St. Boniface

SUNDAY **JUNE 6**

10TH SUNDAY *in* ORDINARY TIME

The readings today remind us of our eternal home, our destiny—the eternal glory that awaits us in heaven. Our human journey on this earth is temporary and just like upon any journey, we get weary, dusty, and at some points we reach exhaustion. We constantly need refreshment, cleansing, and we need our energies to be restored. The "kindness" and the "plenteous redemption" that the Psalmist speaks of are our hope for renewal.

We have a gift of our Christian faith which frames our lives and our actions. Our faith in God has the power to redeem us to the extent that we allow ourselves to trust in him. Where sometimes it seems easier to try to settle for comforts that provide temporary solutions, we eventually realize that only God can heal us into complete wholeness. Our faith grows as we grow. Faith is not meant to remain stagnant; faith needs to grow, to reach new depths.

To be a part of God's family, we need not do something extraordinary or special. All that God asks of us is that we follow God's will. God's eternal home is open to everyone in equal measure, regardless of their status, or religious or cultural identity, so that "the grace bestowed in abundance on more and more people may cause the thanksgiving to overflow for the glory of God."

NATALIA KONONENKO

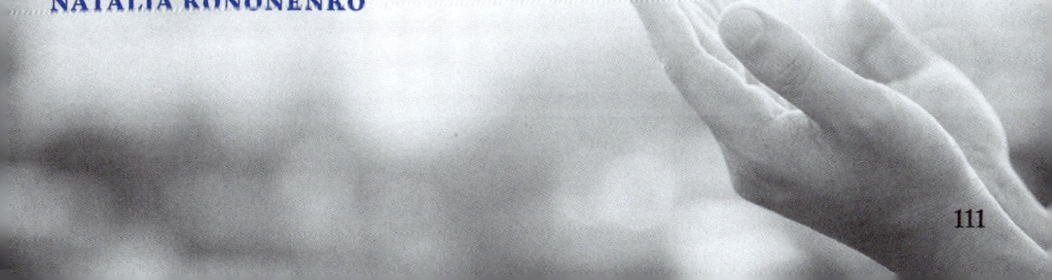

Responding *to the* Word

The Christian prays as a member of the family of Jesus. ***What can I do to be more receptive to God's will for me?***

PEOPLE AND PRAYERS TO REMEMBER THIS WEEK

READINGS OF THE DAY

Genesis 3:9-15

Psalm 130

2 Corinthians 4:13–5:1

Mark 3:20-35

Final Thoughts...

FEASTS THIS WEEK

June 9: **St. Ephrem**

June 11: **St. Barnabas**

11TH SUNDAY *in* ORDINARY TIME

If a small farmer in Puerto Rico wants a fence that will last, a strong limb from a roble tree will do the job. The branch once placed in a post hole along a fence line will come alive in the moist tropical soil. New growth will soon appear on the seemingly dead post. It will grow into a sturdy tree which will resist rot and decay.

Life can be held in a piece of wood or the most insignificant seed. The Bible offers us parables: the cedar twig spoken of by the prophet Ezekiel, the grain of wheat and the mustard seed in Mark's gospel. They show us that the kingdom of God can come alive in our world from the most insignificant of things.

A simple act of kindness to a stranger, standing up to give witness against an injustice, or handing a warm bowl of soup to a hungry person may be the small act that plants the seed of the kingdom in another person's heart. Christianity itself took root from a small community of women and men fearfully huddled together in an upper room after the crucifixion. Jesus, their teacher, was seen by the authorities as just an itinerant preacher from Galilee whose teachings caused them trouble. Today, Christians account for a full third of the world's population. Confidently scattering its seeds, we know the kingdom grows around us. **MICHAEL DOUGHERTY**

PEOPLE AND PRAYERS TO REMEMBER THIS WEEK

Responding *to the* Word

All on earth is under the rule of God, who can "bring low the high tree, lift high the lowly tree." ***What situations in life make me forget how truly powerful God is?***

READINGS OF THE DAY

Ezekiel 17:22-24

Psalm 92

2 Corinthians 5:6-10

Mark 4:26-34

Final Thoughts...

FEASTS THIS WEEK

June 19: **St. Romuald**

SUNDAY **JUNE 20**

12TH SUNDAY *in* ORDINARY TIME

Today's gospel is about faith in Jesus, and how our human fears, like those of the apostles, weaken our faith. What do we fear? Losing our job? A death in the family? A broken marriage?

The apostles are in a boat with Jesus when a violent squall comes and waves break over the boat. Fearing for their lives, they awaken Jesus, asleep in the stern, and ask: "Teacher, do you not care that we are perishing?" After calming the wind and the waves, he asks in return, "Why are you terrified? Do you not yet have faith?"

Like the apostles, how often do we fail to recognize Jesus' presence when our lives are buffeted by adversity? It is only our belief in Jesus that enables us to weather the storms that wreak havoc in our lives. At such times, we have a choice: to seek Jesus through prayer or to lose hope. How strong is our faith? How strong is our hope in prayer? How focused are our eyes on the person of Jesus?

Fear challenges us; faith sustains us. Faith is nourished through developing a relationship with Jesus: faith is the source of hope. Without faith, we, like the apostles, find ourselves threatened by the stormy waters that surround our lives. Faith in Jesus enables us to say with the apostles, "Who then is this whom even wind and sea obey?" **SR. JOHANNA D'AGOSTINO, I.B.V.M.**

PEOPLE AND PRAYERS TO REMEMBER THIS WEEK

Responding *to the* Word

Paul changes how he evaluates people now that he sees them "in Christ." ***How has the reality that each person is beloved by Christ changed the way I think of others?***

READINGS OF THE DAY

Job 38:1, 8-11

Psalm 107

2 Corinthians 5:14-17

Mark 4:35-41

Final Thoughts...

FEASTS THIS WEEK

June 21: **St. Aloysius Gonzaga**

June 22: **St. Paulinus of Nola**
St. John Fisher & St. Thomas More

June 24: **Nativity of St. John the Baptist**

SUNDAY **JUNE 27**

13TH SUNDAY *in* ORDINARY TIME

We often express gratitude for our faith; yet today's readings invite us to reflect on how profoundly that faith influences our view of the world, our actions and ourselves.

Creation is holy, the Wisdom writer suggests—"wholesome." And we, "formed...to be imperishable," made in the image of God's "own nature," are infused with the divine. We are in constant relationship with a God of wonder who transforms us, heals us, turning our "mourning into dancing." "Do not be afraid; just have faith," says Jesus to an anxious father. A woman isolated through illness hears, "Daughter, your faith has saved you. Go in peace and be cured of your affliction." Faith, Jesus says, is everything: it allows the seemingly impossible.

Holiness. Relationship. Healing. Transformation. All seem connected in the vision of faith fashioned in today's readings. A faith grounded in beauty and wonder challenges us to treat the earth and each other as precious. A faith enlivened by the Holy Spirit invites our participation in the mission of Jesus, of God who embraced our humanity.

With Jesus, we are invited to build the kingdom through loving encounter. Faith invites us to consider possibilities: to act in hope affirming the holy, the wondrous; to commit to the seemingly impossible as agents of transformation in our time and place. At the heart of our faith we meet a God who urges us to recognize the holiness that is, while working toward what might be. **ELLA ALLEN**

PEOPLE AND PRAYERS TO REMEMBER THIS WEEK

READINGS OF THE DAY

Wisdom 1:13-15; 2:23-24

Psalm 30

2 Corinthians 8:7, 9, 13-15

Mark 5:21-43

Responding *to the* Word

God created us for life and shared the divine life with us. ***When have I most felt God's life-giving power at work in me?***

Final Thoughts...

FEASTS THIS WEEK

June 28: **St. Irenaeus**

June 29: **St. Peter & St. Paul**

June 30: **First Martyrs of the Holy Roman Church**

July 1: **St. Junípero Serra**

July 3: **St. Thomas**

SUNDAY **JULY 4**

14TH SUNDAY *in* ORDINARY TIME

It can be hard to be a prophet, especially to acquaintances. In today's gospel, the people of Jesus' hometown reject him. They think they know him. They have pigeonholed Jesus, the son of Mary, as a simple carpenter. When Jesus defies their expectations of him, they become defensive. Like the Israelites of Ezekiel's day, they are stubborn: they refuse to accept God's word. Although their lack of faith amazes him, Jesus remains faithful to his mission, proclaiming the kingdom of God among the villages.

We may not consider ourselves prophets; yet because we have been baptized into the life of Christ, we share in the prophetic role. In a unique way, we are all prophets in the hometown spaces of our daily life. Whenever we are faithful to the gospel's message, we are prophets to our families, friends, co-workers, and communities. We may grow disheartened if family members abandon the Church. We may become discouraged if others reject the message and criticize us. We may stumble and doubt ourselves. This is when the sufficiency of God's grace, so powerful for Paul in his struggles, emboldens us to carry on in fidelity.

In this eucharistic celebration, let us give thanks for the grace, for the life of Christ dwelling within us, that gives us the courage to be hometown prophets. **LOUISE MCEWAN**

PEOPLE AND PRAYERS TO REMEMBER THIS WEEK

Responding *to the* Word

Ezekiel is commanded to prophesy even though his audience will be unreceptive. ***What gives me the courage to go on when others are unreceptive to my witness?***

READINGS OF THE DAY

Ezekiel 2:2-5

Psalm 123

2 Corinthians 12:7-10

Mark 6:1-6a

Final Thoughts...

FEASTS THIS WEEK

July 5: **St. Anthony Zaccaria**
St. Elizabeth of Portugal

July 6: **St. Maria Goretti**

July 9: **St. Augustine Zhao Rong & Companions**

15TH SUNDAY *in* ORDINARY TIME

There are people who say: "The Church needs to be prophetic!" or with some nostalgia: "Where have the prophets gone?" It is true that we are in great need of prophetic voices: peace is jeopardized in so many countries of the world; mistrust and intolerance are creating barriers between religious groups; and the future seems to be doom and gloom for so many. Prophets of peace, justice, understanding, and hope would indeed be more than welcome in our times.

But who says there are no prophets among us? The problem might rather be that we fail to recognize them and to hear their message. For prophets are disturbing people. They are constantly challenging us. And who really wants to be disturbed or challenged?

Prophets like Amos are closely tied to a people, a region, a society, whom they cherish and for whose future they care so much. And yet people like him are perceived as disturbers. They find themselves often in hostile territory. We like to have prophets, but are we willing to listen to these prophets who live among us?

Jesus, while sending his own disciples to proclaim the good news of a loving and caring God, understands they will find opposition, mistrust, and even rejection. Are there any prophets still? Or would the question be: do we listen to prophetic voices among us? People who dare to challenge us. People who dare to plead for justice, care, and compassion. People who dare to dream of peace, tolerance, and mutual respect among nations. Such people do exist. The only question now is: when are we going to take them seriously and start building the world according to their dream? JEAN-PIERRE PRÉVOST

PEOPLE AND PRAYERS TO REMEMBER THIS WEEK

Responding *to the* **Word**

Paul reminds us that God has chosen us, adopted us, and lavished many gifts on us. ***For what gifts am I especially thankful today?***

READINGS OF THE DAY

Amos 7:12-15

Psalm 85

Ephesians 1:3-14

Mark 6:7-13

Final Thoughts...

FEASTS THIS WEEK

July 13: **St. Henry**

July 14: **St. Kateri Tekakwitha**

July 15: **St. Bonaventure**

July 16: **Our Lady of Mount Carmel**

SUNDAY **JULY 18**

16TH SUNDAY *in* ORDINARY TIME

Today's gospel tells us that Jesus and the apostles needed to rest. The apostles had just returned from their mission, and Jesus knew they would all benefit from time to renew themselves. But the people, desperate to be with Jesus, made their way to where Jesus was going even before Jesus' boat arrived. What is it about Jesus that kept drawing these crowds to him?

When Jesus saw the crowds, he had compassion for them. Compassion is the ability to feel for others and to love them in a deep, caring way. Jesus was tired—this was supposed to be his time alone with the apostles. Nevertheless, he tended to the needs of the crowd. Jesus had a reputation for such compassion. Here, he reached out first to the apostles, who had not even had time to eat, and then to the people who were like sheep without a shepherd. Imagine how wonderful it must have been to experience this kind of caring and gentle mercy.

I am grateful for today's reading. It reminds me that I am a member of this persistent crowd, seeking and finding Jesus Christ. Jesus' great compassion is found in the Eucharist, where he teaches us what it means to give of ourselves, even when the task seems overwhelming. Let us give thanks for the celebration of the Eucharist, where we find the compassion and love that we need in order to be compassionate to others. **BETH MCISAAC BRUCE**

Responding *to the* Word

Jesus felt compassion for those who wanted so badly to find God. ***What might I do this week to help others in their search for God?***

PEOPLE AND PRAYERS TO REMEMBER THIS WEEK

READINGS OF THE DAY

Jeremiah 23:1-6

Psalm 23

Ephesians 2:13-18

Mark 6:30-34

Final Thoughts...

FEASTS THIS WEEK

July 20: **St. Apollinaris**

July 21: **St. Lawrence of Brindisi**

July 22: **St. Mary Magdalene**

July 23: **St. Bridget**

July 24: **St. Sharbel Makhlūf**

SUNDAY **JULY 25**

17TH SUNDAY *in* ORDINARY TIME

World Day for Grandparents & the Elderly

Some 20 years ago I visited a remote mountain village in the Philippines. The people were very poor, subsisting for the most part on rice and fish. With the kind of hospitality that is common in rural communities all over the world, they invited us to join them for a meal. No effort was spared to prepare a feast for the visitors. We dined on boiled water buffalo, tiny live fish still cold from the waters of the mountain stream, heaping bowls of rice, and the greens from some kind of local vegetation. We ate until we were satisfied. Then the food was shared with all of the women, men, and children of the tribe in what became a huge celebration.

I think of this experience whenever I read today's gospel story. With thousands of people gathered on a hillside to hear him speak, Jesus makes a simple request: share a few fish and barley loaves among the crowd. When the people have finished eating, there is an abundance of food left over.

People in Jesus' day regarded this as a miracle, a sign of God's power and infinite goodness. And so it is—for Jesus does something truly wonderful. By his example, he invites everyone to look at the resources they have and share them with others. Jesus reveals us to ourselves. We quite rightly stand in awe of a God who knows us so well that he can call us to be the best that we can be. **SUSAN EATON**

Responding *to the* Word

Elisha is not worried that sharing will exhaust his resources. ***When have I experienced unexpected generosity to me after I have been generous with others?***

PEOPLE AND PRAYERS TO REMEMBER
THIS WEEK

READINGS
OF THE DAY

2 Kings 4:42-44

Psalm 145

Ephesians 4:1-6

John 6:1-15

Final Thoughts...

FEASTS THIS WEEK

July 26: **St. Joachim & St. Anne**

July 29: **St. Martha, St. Mary, & St. Lazarus**

July 30: **St. John Chrysologus**

July 31: **St. Ignatius of Loyola**

SUNDAY **AUGUST 1**

18TH SUNDAY *in* ORDINARY TIME

If there has ever been a generation that demands proof of existence for everything, it must be ours. With our scientific mindset we think we can define reality by what can be proven in a laboratory. Even the Israelites in the desert, however much they complained to Moses, did not demand the visible signs that our culture does. When Moses told them that the bread and the meat showering down on them were gifts from God, the Israelites believed him. Our people today in this fast-paced technological age would have laughed at Moses for this kind of explanation.

If this is truly so, and if this is how we limit what is real, we are the impoverished ones. For as we insist on material proof of life's essentials, our hearts cry out in protest. As we pour our efforts into achieving material comfort, our souls thirst for what cannot be seen and our hearts desire what cannot be proved in laboratories. When a mother reassures her son, "I will stay right here while you go to sleep," she feeds him manna for the soul. Her words carry a love and depth of caring that no technological toy can provide. "Whatever happens, we'll stick together," is manna feeding a discouraged spirit. Jesus' words today, "I am the bread of life," are God's manna, surpassing the need for scientific proof. The "proof" lies in the fact that something deep within us leaps for joy at these words. At last—food that sustains the human spirit, drink that quenches our thirst for God. MARIE-LOUISE TERNIER-GOMMERS

PEOPLE AND PRAYERS TO REMEMBER THIS WEEK

READINGS OF THE DAY

Exodus 16:2-4, 12-15

Psalm 78

Ephesians 4:17, 20-24

John 6:24-35

Responding *to the* Word

Paul encourages us to adopt a new way of life modeled on Christ. ***What might I do to be more like Christ today?***

Final Thoughts...

FEASTS THIS WEEK

August 2: **St. Eusebius of Vercelli**
St. Peter Julian Eymard

August 4: **St. John Vianney**

August 5: **Dedication of the Basilica of St. Mary Major**

August 6: **Transfiguration of the Lord**

August 7: **St. Sixtus II & Companions**
St. Cajetan

SUNDAY **AUGUST 8**

19TH SUNDAY *in* ORDINARY TIME

Food is essential to our continued existence. As is all too often illustrated by the poor and starving of the world, including in our own nation, if we do not eat we will die. That is why physical nourishment is such a powerful image for our spiritual life as well. Just as human bodies die without food, so too the spirit withers if it is not nourished.

The story of Elijah combines both the physical and spiritual aspects of nourishment. Elijah became discouraged in his battle against the pagan idolatry that was creeping into ancient Israel. He had given up and wanted to die. Instead, God sent an angel to feed him real bread, so that he might build up his strength for a 40-day journey to Mount Horeb. Horeb, which is another name for Mount Sinai, was the place where God first revealed the covenant to the Israelites. By taking Elijah back to the source of Israelite religion, the Lord will renew his spirit, but first he must prepare his body for the journey.

In today's gospel, Jesus uses bread as a symbol for spiritual nourishment, but his audience does not understand. They can only think of manna, the miraculous bread that God sent their ancestors in the desert. However, Jesus himself is the bread that feeds the soul, sent by the Father for their nourishment.

We today face the same challenge, namely, to see beyond the symbol of bread to the reality it expresses. As it was in Jesus' day, so too today: those who eat his body will feed their souls and gain everlasting life. **JOHN L. MCLAUGHLIN**

PEOPLE AND PRAYERS TO REMEMBER THIS WEEK

Responding *to the* Word

Elijah was nourished by God when he thought his troubles were too great. ***How has God strengthened me in times of trouble?***

READINGS OF THE DAY

1 Kings 19:4-8

Psalm 34

Ephesians 4:30–5:2

John 6:41-51

Final Thoughts...

FEASTS THIS WEEK

August 9: **St. Teresa Benedicta of the Cross**

August 10: **St. Lawrence**

August 11: **St. Clare**

August 12: **St. Jane Frances de Chantal**

August 13: **St. Pontian & St. Hippolytus**

August 14: **St. Maximilian Kolbe**

SUNDAY **AUGUST 15**

THE ASSUMPTION *of the* BLESSED VIRGIN MARY

In today's gospel reading, we read about Mary visiting Elizabeth and we hear Mary's famous song of praise, the Magnificat. What is the significance of this reading that we have become so accustomed to hearing? In short, it is a concise summary of God's plan of salvation.

Mary gives praise to God for looking with favor upon her lowliness, for showing mercy for those who fear him, filling the hungry with good things, and, conversely, for bringing down the powerful and essentially restoring a sense of justice in the world. If ever it seems that our world is out of order, as it often does, this song of praise serves as a stark reminder that justice will prevail.

Mary's song of praise is also a reminder that things may not be what they seem on the surface. Mary, the young, unwed mother-to-be, became an outcast in the eyes of her society. Had anyone imagined the special mission God had given her in life?

Perhaps the person in our midst who often seems a nuisance to those around, who might be difficult to get along with, who simply does not fit in with the general standard of approval—perhaps that person too has a special relationship with God and a special mission in life. Who are we to judge? NATALIA KONONENKO

PEOPLE AND PRAYERS TO REMEMBER THIS WEEK

READINGS OF THE DAY

Revelation 11:19a; 12:1-6a, 10ab

Psalm 45

1 Corinthians 15:20-27

Luke 1:39-56

Responding *to the* Word

Mary praises God for his marvelous deeds. ***When has God surprised me in my life in a powerful way?***

Final Thoughts...

FEASTS THIS WEEK

August 16: **St. Stephen of Hungary**
August 19: **St. John Eudes**
August 20: **St. Bernard**
August 21: **St. Pius X**

SUNDAY **AUGUST 22**

21ST SUNDAY *in* ORDINARY TIME

Jesus doesn't tell people what they want to hear. He speaks the truth without waffling, capitulating, or justifying. Truth is what it is.

Many followers, both in that moment and for generations after, abandon Jesus because they simply cannot accept his words. Maybe the truth does not jibe with their "truth," maybe it is too difficult, or perhaps they can't trust in what they don't understand. Whatever the reason, they opt out.

Then Jesus turns to his disciples, his friends, the men who've walked with him, and asks, "Do you also want to leave?" Imagine that. After all they'd been through together, after all he'd shown and taught them, he lays the choice before them.

Today, he lays it before us. As for me and my household, we will serve...what fills that blank? Better yet, what fills our time? What fills our thoughts? We'd like it to be the Lord. But is it, really?

Choosing to serve the Lord doesn't happen just once. It's a daily decision made in how we live our lives in the moment, how we love each other now, how we spend our time and talents today. Just as Joshua challenged the tribes, just as Jesus challenged his disciples all those generations ago, we too are challenged to make our choice. Today, let us make it wholeheartedly. **CAROLINE PIGNAT**

PEOPLE AND PRAYERS TO REMEMBER THIS WEEK

Responding *to the* Word

Paul encourages us to live in love, which creates the kind of community that God wants. ***What loving practices can I do this week to build community with others?***

READINGS OF THE DAY

Joshua 24:1-2a, 15-17, 18b

Psalm 34

Ephesians 5:21-32 or 5:2a, 25-32

John 6:60-69

Final Thoughts...

FEASTS THIS WEEK

August 23: **St. Rose of Lima**

August 24: **St. Bartholomew**

August 25: **St. Louis**
St. Joseph Calasanz

August 27: **St. Monica**

August 28: **St. Augustine**

SUNDAY **AUGUST 29**

22ND SUNDAY *in* ORDINARY TIME

Today we are offered two very different visions of right living before God. One is to blindly follow the letter of the law; the other is to follow its heart. It is tempting in daily life to hold others to the letter of the law and ourselves to the spirit of the law.

A quick glance at the first reading might lead us to think that God demands blind obedience. But there is no room for wisdom, intelligence, and discernment in blind obedience, and this passage treasures them. Deuteronomy warns against changing the law. Wisdom, intelligence, and discernment are gifts of the Holy Spirit. They do not change the law; rather, they seek its heart.

God's gift is the law; our duty to the gift is to follow in wisdom and discernment. As Jesus points out to the Pharisees, these gifts dwell in the human heart—strangely enough, right alongside evil thoughts and intentions. In the second reading James tells us that when God's gifts take root in our hearts, our actions on behalf of others bear witness to this truth.

Each Sunday, the Holy Spirit stirs and transforms our hearts. The texts of the Sunday celebration are shot through with God's "heart" language: love, mercy, peace, forgiveness. Let us tune our ears today to hear this heart language in the liturgy. Let us allow the Holy Spirit to teach us heart language in our daily lives. MARGARET BICK

PEOPLE AND PRAYERS TO REMEMBER THIS WEEK

READINGS OF THE DAY

Deuteronomy 4:1-2, 6-8

Psalm 15

James 1:17-18, 21b-22, 27

Mark 7:1-8, 14-15, 21-23

Responding *to the* Word

Jesus warns that the real roots of sin are our inner attitudes. ***What attitude is giving me trouble lately and pushing me toward wrong actions?***

Final Thoughts...

FEASTS THIS WEEK

September 3: **St. Gregory the Great**

SUNDAY **SEPTEMBER 5**

23RD SUNDAY *in* ORDINARY TIME

When Jesus heals the deaf man in today's gospel, he is clearly fulfilling what had been prophesied by the prophet Isaiah: that when God comes, the ears of the deaf will be unstopped and the speechless will sing for joy. This is all well and good for the deaf fellow 2,000 years ago, we might ask ourselves, but what does it matter to us today?

One way to reflect on today's readings is to consider the ways in which I myself am deaf and mute to the presence of God in my life: how I am too distracted to hear the beautiful sounds of creation; too preoccupied to pay attention to the goodness, the love, and the wisdom of others; too busy to listen to what the Word of God is saying to me in my day-to-day life.

We believe that because of the life, death, and resurrection of Jesus, God truly is present in our world and in our lives; this is what is being pointed to when Jesus heals the deaf man in today's gospel.

Let us, therefore, listen attentively for God's presence in our lives, in the Scriptures, and in the Eucharist. For the more we come to know God's love for us, the more will we, like the speechless in Isaiah, sing for joy—bringing this loving presence of God to our families, friends, and communities. **REV. ARMAND MERCIER**

PEOPLE AND PRAYERS TO REMEMBER THIS WEEK

Responding *to the* Word

Isaiah encourages us to "Be strong, fear not!" because God is with us. ***When has God's presence helped calm my fears?***

READINGS OF THE DAY

Isaiah 35:4-7a

Psalm 146

James 2:1-5

Mark 7:31-37

Final Thoughts...

FEASTS THIS WEEK

September 8: **Nativity of the Blessed Virgin Mary**

September 9: **St. Peter Claver**

SUNDAY **SEPTEMBER 12**

24TH SUNDAY *in* ORDINARY TIME

In today's gospel, we have Peter's confession of faith. But what is faith? Is it nothing more than believing in an idea?

Peter says that Jesus is the Christ, but when Jesus teaches that he must suffer and be put to death, Peter rejects this. Peter is looking for a winner. Jesus sounds like a loser to Peter, so Peter must make Jesus into his understanding of a winner.

Like Peter, how often do we try to make over Jesus into our image? Often, we try to make Jesus into someone we think he should be, instead of taking Jesus for who he is.

The way of Jesus is to lose yourself, to let go and be in God. Belief in God is more than assent to abstract concepts. It is a relationship with someone and, in relationships, we have to give something of ourselves to grow with the other.

Saint James tells us that faith alone will not save anyone, but faith must manifest itself in relationships. Pope Francis reminded us time and again that relationships are the key to a life of faith. Doctrine without people at its heart is not good teaching. As we prepare to celebrate the Eucharist today, let us ask for the courage to accept Jesus as he is and not as we want him to be. **ANTHONY CHEZZI**

PEOPLE AND PRAYERS TO REMEMBER THIS WEEK

Responding *to the* Word

God's servant must put up with hardship to do what God asks. ***How do I respond to hardship and difficulties in living as God requires?***

READINGS OF THE DAY

Isaiah 50:4c-9a

Psalm 116

James 2:14-18

Mark 8:27-35

Final Thoughts...

FEASTS THIS WEEK

September 13: **St. John Chrysostom**

September 14: **Exaltation of the Holy Cross**

September 15: **Our Lady of Sorrows**

September 16: **St. Cornelius & St. Cyprian**

September 17: **St. Robert Bellarmine**
St. Hildegard of Bingen

SUNDAY **SEPTEMBER 19**

25TH SUNDAY *in* **ORDINARY TIME**

When I was a young boy, I secretly wished—against all the evidence—that everyone would think I was the best player on our baseball team. I also had the secret desire that one day my teacher would say, "You are the best student in the class. In fact, you are the best student I have ever had!" Now, of course, I have put such juvenile fantasies behind me. Although, I have to admit, I would love to see a billboard that said, "Best Dad ever!" with my photograph. So, it's oddly comforting to read today that Jesus' twelve closest friends and disciples were not above squabbling over who was the greatest of them all.

Jesus' response is both reassuring and challenging. He did not criticize them for their pride or self-delusion. Instead, he looked deep into their hearts and responded to what he saw there—their idealism, their desire to do good, their wish to be his faithful followers. He simply ignored the immature way it showed itself.

Jesus showed them that the way to Christian greatness is simple. You don't need a golden halo, or the skills to explain profound theological insights, or a wardrobe full of sackcloth and ashes. The way is as close as the person right beside you, right here, right now. Truly and deeply welcome that person, in all their messy humanity, as Jesus truly and deeply welcomes us. **PATRICK GALLAGHER**

PEOPLE AND PRAYERS TO REMEMBER THIS WEEK

READINGS OF THE DAY

Wisdom 2:12, 17-20

Psalm 54

James 3:16–4:3

Mark 9:30-37

Responding *to the* Word

Jesus bluntly tells the disciples that their greatness will come only from service. ***What service am I doing that would make Jesus happy?***

Final Thoughts...

FEASTS THIS WEEK

September 20: **St. Andrew Kim Tae-gŏn, St. Paul Chŏng Ha-sang, & Companions**

September 21: **St. Matthew**

September 23: **St. Pius of Pietrelcina**

SUNDAY **SEPTEMBER 26**

26TH SUNDAY *in* ORDINARY TIME

World Day of Migrants & Refugees

How many times have people been stereotyped and even excluded when we have heard or thought, "but they are not one of us"? Today, we are presented with two instances in which the followers of Moses and Jesus fail to grasp that the Spirit of the Lord has no limits and is certainly not under their control.

The apostles did not understand Jesus' inclusive love and outreach. While Moses recognized the Spirit, he understood that not everyone did: "Would that all the people of the LORD were prophets! Would that the LORD might bestow his spirit on them all!"

But we are born into a world in which the Spirit of God is already at work. Saint John Paul II affirmed that the Spirit of God is both God's presence and activity in the world.

Jesus invites us all to live with reverence for a missionary God who moves and acts in ways unknown to us—and to do so with openness and respect for all creation. Our primary responsibility is to prayerfully discern God's presence and how to be faithful today to our baptismal commitment. Jesus gives us a fundamental guideline for both our discernment and discipleship: "Whoever is not against us is for us." **REV. JACK LYNCH, S.F.M.**

Responding *to the* Word

God's Spirit can empower the most unlikely people. ***What unlikely "prophet" surprised me as one from whom I learned much about God?***

PEOPLE AND PRAYERS TO REMEMBER
THIS WEEK

READINGS
OF THE DAY

Numbers 11:25-29

Psalm 19

James 5:1-6

Mark 9:38-43, 45, 47-48

Final Thoughts...

FEASTS THIS WEEK

September 27: **St. Vincent de Paul**

September 28: **St. Wenceslaus**
St. Lawrence Ruiz & Companions

September 29: **St. Michael, St. Gabriel,**
& St. Raphael

September 30: **St. Jerome**

October 1: **St. Thérèse of the Child Jesus**

October 2: **Holy Guardian Angels**

SUNDAY **OCTOBER 3**

27TH SUNDAY *in* ORDINARY TIME

Jesus regularly spoke of the ideals to which God calls us, rather than the accommodations we often make. His teaching on divorce is an example of that. In keeping with his usual approach, he challenged the Pharisees to aim for God's original plan for marriage, even though the Law allowed for divorce.

God's plan for male-female relationships is illustrated by the first reading. Life in the garden was incomplete because the first human did not have a partner. Humans are meant to be in relationships with others, not alone and isolated. God made the animals, but none was an appropriate "partner" because the Hebrew word actually means "one like himself." So, God took part of that first human and made it into a suitable partner. This story illustrates God's plan for marriage, that a man and a woman find a part of themselves in the other and therefore devote themselves exclusively to the other.

Unfortunately, humans did not remain in the ideal creation that was the Garden of Eden. Because of sin, they had to leave the garden and were forced to live a much harsher existence. In the world we live in today, relationships sometimes break down. When that happens, we need to attend to the pastoral needs of those involved while keeping in view the ideal of God's original plan that Jesus evokes in today's gospel. **JOHN L. MCLAUGHLIN**

PEOPLE AND PRAYERS TO REMEMBER THIS WEEK

READINGS OF THE DAY

Genesis 2:18-24

Psalm 128

Hebrews 2:9-11

Mark 10:2-16

Responding *to the* **Word**

God recognized that being alone is not very good for humans. ***What might I do this week to make sure that someone does not feel so alone?***

Final Thoughts...

FEASTS THIS WEEK

October 4: **St. Francis of Assisi**

October 5: **St. Faustina Kowalska**
Bl. Francis Xavier Seelos

October 6: **St. Bruno**
Bl. Marie Rose Durocher

October 7: **Our Lady of the Rosary**

October 9: **St. Denis & Companions**
St. John Leonardi
St. John Henry Newman

SUNDAY **OCTOBER 10**

28TH SUNDAY *in* ORDINARY TIME

I remember racing home from school with my report card, blazing with great marks. After careful scrutiny, my dad would say there was still room for improvement. Today's gospel brings that memory back. I know that my dad was very proud of me, yet he was challenging me to be better.

When the rich young man eagerly approaches Jesus, he wants to make Jesus aware that he has lived a good life, for he has followed the commandments. Jesus "loved him" and then challenged him to do more, to be better, to use his wealth to help others as his journey to salvation. The rich young man's "face fell, and he went away sad." Jesus was asking more than he could do.

The Jewish people saw wealth as a sign of favor from God. In fact, it is the gift of salvation that is a sign of God's favor—for "all things are possible for God."

Jesus' words demonstrate that the commandments are meant as a framework for our faith; we are called to go beyond "you shall not" and open ourselves to "you shall." Faith fully lived is a call to action in our daily lives. Our riches, whether material wealth, talents, or time, are meant to be shared with others.

We have often heard that God loves a cheerful giver. Will we give cheerfully, or will we walk away? **SUSAN BERLINGERI**

PEOPLE AND PRAYERS TO REMEMBER THIS WEEK

Responding *to the* Word

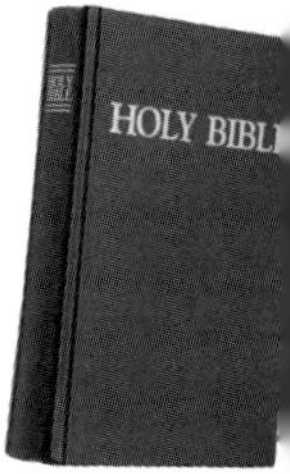

God's word can penetrate deep into our inner self and reveal things we might not want to see. ***When has God's word in Scripture revealed surprising depths about me and about God?***

READINGS OF THE DAY

Wisdom 7:7-11

Psalm 90

Hebrews 4:12-13

Mark 10:17-30

Final Thoughts...

FEASTS THIS WEEK

October 11: **St. John XXIII**

October 12: **St. Carlo Acutis**

October 14: **St. Callistus I**

October 15: **St. Teresa of Jesus**

October 16: **St. Hedwig**
St. Margaret Mary Alacoque

SUNDAY **OCTOBER 17**

29TH SUNDAY *in* ORDINARY TIME

Today, Jesus' disciples provide a remarkable display of pride, envy, squabbling, and spitefulness. James and John want Jesus to make them Disciples #1 and #1A, and they show no doubt whatsoever that they can easily meet the job requirements. When the other disciples catch wind of this request, they start to complain and demand their own elevation to lofty status. It's not a very edifying scene.

Somehow, I always find it encouraging when people who are thought of as holy or spiritually advanced show the human weaknesses with which I am all too familiar. It reminds me that Jesus can work with the most imperfect and flawed raw material, like a potter can work with clay. With strong and skillful hands, he smooths out the rough and damaged parts. With insight and love, he sees the unique strength and worth of what his hands are holding. With tenderness and patience, he waits for the inner beauty and intrinsic value of what he is working with to reveal itself.

Jesus knew what he had. He knew these weak and flawed men had it in them to inspire others and to lead in spreading the good news throughout the world. They just needed a little help.
If Jesus can work with them, then surely, he can work with us. **PATRICK GALLAGHER**

PEOPLE AND PRAYERS TO REMEMBER THIS WEEK

READINGS OF THE DAY

Isaiah 53:10-11

Psalm 33

Hebrews 4:14-16

Mark 10:35-45

Responding *to the* Word

Through suffering, God's servant helps many others. ***How has my suffering made me more ready to help others who suffer?***

Final Thoughts...

FEASTS THIS WEEK

October 18: **St. Luke**

October 19: **St. John de Brébeuf, St. Isaac Jogues, & Companions**

October 20: **St. Paul of the Cross**

October 22: **St. John Paul II**

October 23: **St. John of Capistrano**

SUNDAY **OCTOBER 24**

30TH SUNDAY *in* ORDINARY TIME

World Mission Sunday

In today's gospel, we encounter Bartimaeus, the blind beggar, sitting at the side of the road as Jesus makes his way to Jerusalem. The road is crowded with people talking excitedly and jostling for position, hoping to get close to Jesus. Bartimaeus, hearing that Jesus is passing by, calls out loudly and insistently until Jesus responds. When Jesus calls, Bartimaeus enthusiastically throws off his cloak, springs up, and comes to Jesus.

Because of his blindness, Bartimaeus needs others to lead him through the noisy, chaotic throng of people. On his own, Bartimaeus is unable to find Jesus; he comes to Jesus through others. Changed by his encounter with Jesus, Bartimaeus follows him on the way to Jerusalem and to his Passion.

"The way" is another name for discipleship. Following Jesus leads to communion with others and engagement with the world, regardless of the cost. If our faith sits at the roadside, looking blindly inward, it lacks the intentionality of discipleship. Faith that enthusiastically gets up in response to Jesus' call restores both us and the community. Discipleship is a road traveled through the events of a lifetime.

In the first reading, God promises to gather the broken. We celebrate today's Eucharist knowing that this promise is fulfilled in Jesus, who calls us out of blindness to discipleship. We celebrate as individuals in community, restored by the great high priest whose way is love. **LOUISE MCEWAN**

PEOPLE AND PRAYERS TO REMEMBER THIS WEEK

Responding *to the* Word

Jesus helps a blind man to see. ***For what do I need Jesus' help to "see" more clearly about my life today?***

READINGS OF THE DAY

Jeremiah 31:7-9

Psalm 126

Hebrews 5:1-6

Mark 10:46-52

Final Thoughts...

FEASTS THIS WEEK

October 28: **St. Simon & St. Jude**

SUNDAY **OCTOBER 31**

31ST SUNDAY *in* ORDINARY TIME

The Great Commandment is at the heart of today's readings. We hear it in Deuteronomy and then quoted by Jesus in Mark's gospel. This declaration of God's unity and call to love God with all our being and our neighbor as ourselves is still today central in Jewish worship. It is called the "Shema"—Hebrew for "Hear!"—because God has a message for us that will make the difference between life and death.

The scribe who queried Jesus about the greatest commandment agrees with Jesus: to love God and our neighbor whole-heartedly is the path to life in God's kingdom. But how can we love this way? Most of us are so busy, so distracted, with so much coming at us. How do we even choose our priorities?

Many holy women and men have recommended "falling in love with God." Nothing is more practical, said Fr. Pedro Arrupe, the late Superior General of the Jesuits. Why practical? Because when we are in love, we know our priorities—we know each day how we will devote our time and talents. And when we are in love, we find time to nourish our relationship. Fr. Pedro said: "Fall in love, stay in love, and it will decide everything." Let us sincerely seek the quiet we need to hear God's love for us, opening ourselves to love and follow God passionately. All else will follow. **BETH PORTER**

PEOPLE AND PRAYERS TO REMEMBER THIS WEEK

Responding *to the* Word

Moses encourages us to love God as completely as we can. ***What can I do this week to strengthen my love for God?***

READINGS OF THE DAY

Deuteronomy 6:2-6

Psalm 18

Hebrews 7:23-28

Mark 12:28b-34

Final Thoughts...

FEASTS THIS WEEK

November 1: **All Saints**

November 2: **All Souls' Day**

November 3: **St. Martin de Porres**

November 4: **St. Charles Borromeo**

MONDAY **NOVEMBER 1**

ALL SAINTS

The feast of All Saints is an occasion to remember and honor the women and men, known and unknown, who lived courageous lives with an unwavering faith in Jesus Christ.

I tend to regard the saints as a distinct group of individuals chosen by God: part of the great multitude, a people set apart. So, when I read a statement by Mother Teresa that "to be a saint, you have to seriously want to be one," I was taken aback. I felt an invitation, even encouragement, to reflect on what I had chosen—in my life, with my life.

I have come to learn that these women and men struggled with their sinfulness, failures, and life's disappointments. In their relationship with God, they were prone to doubts, confusion, selfishness, and even anger. In other words, they were very much like us. Yet, despite their limitations and imperfections, they never gave up on saying "yes" to Christ. They continued to say "no" to worldly values and concerns. The saints, it seems, would not serve two masters.

They strove to be faithful to the kind of life the Beatitudes urge us to live—even to death. The saints' lives reveal that each of us is being called to live our life as a child of God, caring for peace, reconciliation, and the poor. What will our response be to God's invitation? **JULIE CACHIA**

PEOPLE AND PRAYERS TO REMEMBER THIS WEEK

Responding *to the* Word

John has a heavenly vision of all the saints. ***Which saints have been particularly helpful as examples for my Christian life?***

READINGS OF THE DAY

Revelation 7:2-4, 9-14

Psalm 24

1 John 3:1-3

Matthew 5:1-12a

Final Thoughts...

SUNDAY **NOVEMBER 7**

32ND SUNDAY *in* ORDINARY TIME

A poor widow puts two small coins into the collection plate. Not much of an event; not much of a donation. However, Jesus immediately sees past her unattractive exterior into her real identity. Jesus loves her, in her poverty and in her radiance.

Though neither materially poor nor widowed, I too am a "poor widow," as perhaps are you. Like yours, my poverty is hidden from sight: my fears, my self-reproach, my doubts about God. I'm a widow insomuch as I'm incomplete and insecure, insomuch as I ache over what and whom I have lost and may now be losing. You, too, are incomplete. Maybe you, too, ache over someone or something you have lost or are now losing.

In my poverty, I want God. I want comfort. In your poverty, what do you want?

Two small coins were "all she had." In the place where I am poor, what do I actually have? I have my desire to find God and to get past my own smallness; my hope that my messy life can become "a new heaven and a new earth," that God really can get light out of darkest dark. In my poverty, I can still act, though vulnerable. At my poorest, I can give God my trust, however shaky it is. Perhaps that shaky trust is all God asks any of us in tasting the riches of the eucharistic banquet. **NANCY MARROCCO**

PEOPLE AND PRAYERS TO REMEMBER THIS WEEK

Responding *to the* Word

Small gifts sometimes reap unexpected rewards. ***When has some small thing I did had unexpectedly good results?***

READINGS OF THE DAY

1 Kings 17:10-16

Psalm 146

Hebrews 9:24-28

Mark 12:38-44

Final Thoughts...

FEASTS THIS WEEK

November 9: **Dedication of the Lateran Basilica**

November 10: **St. Leo the Great**

November 11: **St. Martin of Tours**

November 12: **St. Josaphat**

November 13: **St. Frances Xavier Cabrini**

SUNDAY **NOVEMBER 14**

33RD SUNDAY *in* ORDINARY TIME

World Day of the Poor

Today's gospel anticipates dramatic events of the end-times, when, after a time of suffering, the world as we know it will pass away. When I consider some of our global relationships and the state of our planet, I see much suffering. Some of us are wealthy, while many more are very poor. Some have power, and others have no voice. The earth is damaged by pollution and over-consumption. I sometimes wonder if we will ever fully live out God's call to love our neighbors and to be good stewards of creation.

Instead of a message of doom, however, this gospel reading offers hope. It offers a future hope in the second coming of Christ and a present hope in the promise that while heaven and earth will pass away, Christ's words will not. This latter promise is fulfilled even after two thousand years, as the Church continues to proclaim the good news of the kingdom of God, a kingdom of love, compassion, kindness, and mercy.

Even in the midst of suffering humanity and the harm done to creation, the Word of God continues to be alive and active in us. As we wait in hope for the fulfillment of the kingdom of God in Christ's return in glory, let us give thanks for the living Word of God empowering us to respect creation and to build a more just, loving, and peaceful world. BETH MCISAAC BRUCE

PEOPLE AND PRAYERS TO REMEMBER THIS WEEK

READINGS OF THE DAY

Daniel 12:1-3

Psalm 16

Hebrews 10:11-14, 18

Mark 13:24-32

Responding *to the* Word

Jesus' self-sacrifice took away our sins, that is, it put us into the right relationship with God and others. ***What in my relationships with God and others needs my attention most today?***

Final Thoughts...

FEASTS THIS WEEK

November 15: **St. Albert the Great**

November 16: **St. Margaret of Scotland**
St. Gertrude

November 17: **St. Elizabeth of Hungary**

November 18: **Dedication of the Basilicas of St. Peter & St. Paul**
St. Rose Philippine Duchesne

SUNDAY **NOVEMBER 21**

OUR LORD JESUS CHRIST, KING *of the* UNIVERSE (CHRIST THE KING)

World Day of Youth

Sometimes it seems each time we turn on the television, we are bombarded with horrible images—monumental poverty, senseless terrorist attacks, never-ending wars. It's discouraging, to say the least. So, what exactly are we celebrating on today's feast of Christ the King? How do we reconcile what's happening in our world with Jesus' teachings about a kingdom of truth and love and peace? One look at the news is all we need to remind us that God's kingdom is not yet a reality.

It's tempting perhaps to throw our hands up in despair and wonder where God is in all of this. But maybe we need to ask ourselves: what are we doing to make God's kingdom a reality in our own world? Jesus showed us what it means to live as citizens of the kingdom of God. We see it in the way he lived his life and his relationships with others.

And perhaps that's where we need to start as well—in our own lives and relationships. Are our own homes places of love and peace and forgiveness for all who live there? Are they shelters where the sick are cared for, where the hungry are fed, where strangers are welcomed? Staying up all night with a sick child, taking a casserole to someone in mourning, opening our homes to the new neighbor—these are the things that make the kingdom of God a reality.

Each time we celebrate the Eucharist, each time we pray the Lord's Prayer, we pray for the coming of God's kingdom into the world. Today when we celebrate Christ as King, may we be challenged to make that kingdom more of a reality in our own lives. **TERESA WHALEN LUX**

PEOPLE AND PRAYERS TO REMEMBER THIS WEEK

READINGS OF THE DAY

Daniel 7:13-14

Psalm 93

Revelation 1:5-8

John 18:33b-37

Responding *to the* Word

Jesus says that those who belong to his kingdom listen to his voice. ***What might I do to be more attentive to what Jesus is calling me to be and do?***

Final Thoughts...

FEASTS THIS WEEK

November 22: **St. Cecilia**

November 23: **St. Clement I**
St. Columban
Bl. Miguel Agustín Pro

November 24: **St. Andrew Dũng-Lạc & Companions**

November 25: **St. Catherine of Alexandria**
Thanksgiving Day

My Spiritual Journey